AGAINST THE STREAM

AGAINST THE STREAM

A Buddhist Manual for
Spiritual Revolutionaries

NOAH LEVINE

HarperSanFrancisco
A Division of HarperCollinsPublishers

HarperCollins books may be purchased for educational, business, or sales promotional use. For information please write: Special Markets Department, HarperCollins Publishers, 10 East 53rd Street, New York, NY 10022.

HarperCollins Web site: http://www.harpercollins.com
HarperCollins®, ☎®, and HarperSanFrancisco™ are
trademarks of HarperCollins Publishers.

FIRST EDITION

Library of Congress Cataloging-in-Publication Data is available.

ISBN: 978–0–06–073664–4
ISBN-10: 0–06–073664–X

07 08 09 10 11 RRD (H) 10 9 8 7 6 5 4 3 2

Dedicated to all beings everywhere.

May these words bring about more understanding
and less confusion in this world.

CONTENTS

FOREWORD

I t is a strange delight to be asked to comment on our son's hard-fought clarity he shares in this book of well-directed instructions and support for mindfulness practice for a generation awakening to its remarkable potential. Each generation finds its own true voice to describe the process of insight and discovery and the language to share this spiritual revolution. Noah has found his voice; speaking from his heart he touches the heart we all share. We are blessed to know him.

Against the Stream is a navigational chart for the journey upstream. The normal currents lull us to sleep and leave us groggy downstream on a concrete shore or at a loss on our deathbed. The Buddha spoke of "the work to be done" and offered a means to awaken from the stupor of conventional thinking and values. He rejected all that was not genuine and startlingly present. He warned against looking outside ourselves for grace. He knew from self-discovery that grace is our original nature.

A beloved early teacher of mine used to say my thoughts had grown old and stale. That old thinking was impeding my practice and my life force. He said we must go beyond old ways of thinking to experience what is real, and to remember that what is sought is not some imagined perfection but the joy of liberation. So he fed me a progression of remarkable Buddhist writings and fine commentaries, such as Noah's excellent manifesto for a revolution of the spirit, a turning around to face the forces that push us unconsciously downstream against our will, against our better knowing, which lift the heart and open great new realms of thought.

This book relays the difference between theory and practice, between thinking it and actually doing it. My teacher said it was time to wake up. Noah wisely reminds us it is time to stop dying-in-place, time to stop treading water and to start making the effort to save our lives. He calls to us from upstream that seeing clearly buoys the spirit.

Noah is acting as your compass, pointing you toward the potential for liberation. He, like the Buddha (I never thought when he was a teen-monster I would ever utter such words), is not asking anything you cannot accomplish. We are all working at the edge of our possibilities, and there's no one who couldn't use a bit of help along the way. If I had met someone like Noah when I too was a troubled teen, I would have healed sooner.

The Buddha once silently held up a flower before his assembled monks to see who could really see. Most of the monks looked confounded. Only one person "got it," understood that no words could hold the vastness of the spirit that is our birthright. What had occurred was a "silent transmission," a leaping of the spirit from one to another.

From Noah's words and affection so much can be drawn, and in the silent transmission from the space between words to the space between your thoughts is where great truths peek through.

Stephen Levine, 2007

AN INVITATION
TO REVOLUTION

Against the Stream is more than just another book about Buddhist meditation. It is a manifesto and field guide for the front lines of the revolution. It is the culmination of almost two decades of meditative dissonance from the next generation of Buddhists in the West. It is a call to awakening for the sleeping masses.

Wake up: the revolution has already begun; it started 2,500 years ago, when Sid (Siddhartha Gautama, Sid for short) emerged victorious over suffering in the battle with his own mind. But, as most things tend to be with time, the spiritual revolution that Sid started, which we now call Buddhism, has been co-opted by the very aspects of humanity that Sid was trying to dismantle. The causes of suffering and confusion in the form of greed, hatred, and delusion have continued to corrupt the masses and have even crept into the teachings of this revolutionary path.

This book is my attempt to present an introduction to the radical path of awakening as I believe it was originally intended and instructed. I have done my best to leave behind the dogmatic and culturally biased perspectives that have come to be part and parcel of many of the current presentations of Buddhism.

That having been said, I must also admit that my own biases and conditioned experiences will surely color these pages with the unenlightened views and opinions that limit my ability to always see clearly. I have not attempted to be precise or historically correct in my interpretations; rather, I have taken the liberty to share the path to awakening as I have been practicing it and experiencing it from the inside out.

I am convinced that what I have presented in these pages is, for the most part, in line with the oldest recorded teachings of the Buddha, the Theravadan tradition, as preserved and practiced in Sri Lanka, Burma (Myanmar), and Thailand. Many of these teachings I received directly from the unbroken monastic lineage that leads all the way back to the Buddha. But more important is the fact that I have directly experienced these teachings and the transformative effects of this path over approximately two decades of meditative engagement. I have not attempted to present all of the wisdom and compassion of the Buddha in these pages; rather, I have done my best to share teachings and techniques that I believe will lead to the direct experiences of the Buddha's compassionate wisdom.

Against the Stream is my attempt to illuminate the path to freedom as I believe the Buddha intended it to be, as a radical and subversive personal rebellion against the causes of suffering and confusion. We have the ability to effect a great positive change in the world, starting with the training of our own minds and the overcoming of our deluded conditioning. Waking up is not a selfish pursuit of happiness; it is a revolutionary stance, from the inside out, for the benefit of all beings in existence.

May the teachings and techniques in this book inspire you to serve the truth of generosity, kindness, and appreciation and to defy the lies of selfishness, ill will, and jealousy. May all beings meditate and destroy the causes of suffering in the forms of internal and external oppression and ignorance. And may the inner revolution bear the fruit of freedom you took birth to experience!

THE DHARMA PUNX PATH

I came to this path and perspective from a place of deep confusion and great suffering. These teachings are not theoretical or philosophical to me; they have been directly experienced. Although I have already written in detail about my personal experiences of coming to and applying these practices in my memoir, *Dharma Punx,* I offer this abbreviated version for those who are unfamiliar with my story.

In 1988 I woke up in a padded cell, addicted to drugs, committed to a life of crime and violence, and wanting to die. Prior to that day, I had seen myself as a rebel, a punk rock revolutionary. Ever since I was a child I had been engaged in illegal and illicit activity. It seems that I had always known that the material world is run by oppression and ignorance and that the only viable solution is to rebel, to go against the stream. And I had been successful at defying the cultural norms of society's laws and structure—at least externally. I had raised myself on a steady diet of punk rock nihilism and antiauthority ethics in a haze of drug-induced self-destruction.

From an early age I was suicidal. Ironically, drugs and the punk ethic were the very things that allowed me to survive adolescence. In drugs I found temporary freedom from the pain and confusion of life. In punk rock I found meaning, community, and a form in which to express my discontent. At first these things promised freedom and meaning, but by the time I was a teenager, I was losing hope and exchanged my punk ethic for a life of crime and addiction. The years of confusion and a life of following my mind's cravings and anger led to repeated incarcerations and deeper and deeper levels of suffering.

At seventeen years old, after waking up in the padded cell of the local juvenile hall, I could no longer see a way to blame the world for my problems. Instead, I began to see that *I* was the problem. I was the one stealing, taking drugs, and hurting people. I was in jail because of my actions, not because of anyone else's. I had no one to blame but myself. I was overcome with the pain and sorrow that were fueling my downward spiral. My whole life had become a quest to escape from reality.

But this time in juvenile hall, something was different. I could see where I was, and it scared me. It was more real and for the first time in my life, I knew that where I was and what I had become was my fault. I had always blamed everyone else: the cops, the system, society, my teachers, my family: everyone but myself. I was a victim of my surroundings, a product of my environment. But none of that was working anymore. With shocking clarity I could see that my wretched state was the consequence of my addiction to drugs: this is what happens to thieving drug addicts like me.

I had hit bottom. I had lost all hope; death was all I had to look forward to. On the phone with my father, I told him about all the regret and fear I was experiencing. He suggested that some simple meditation techniques might help alleviate some of what I was feeling. He explained to me the basics of meditation and told me that much of the difficulty I was experiencing was due to replaying the events of the past and making up stories about the future. He reminded me that in the present moment I had food to eat, a bed to sleep in, and clothes to wear.

My dad had been telling me things like this my whole life, but I had never really heard him until that day. I had always felt that meditation was a waste of time, the hobby of hippies and New Age weirdos. It had never made sense to me to sit still and meditate. I had always felt that there was too much to do, too much to experience, and perhaps too much pain and confusion to face. Although I was shaking with the fear of spending the rest of my life in prison and physically aching from all of the abuse I had put myself through, I could finally see that he was right. Deep down I wanted to live, and something inside of me knew that meditation was my last hope of survival.

My father said, "The best way to keep the mind in the present moment, in the beginning, is through awareness of breathing." He offered me this simple instruction: "Bring your awareness to the breath by focusing your attention on the sensation of breathing. Attempt to stay with the sensations of each breath by counting each inhalation and exhalation. Try to count to ten—breathing in, one; breathing out, two; and so on. Whenever the mind wanders off to the thoughts of the future or past, gently bring it back to the breath and start over at one. If you can actually stay with the breath all the way to ten, start over again at one."

This turned out to be the beginning of a meditation practice that would prove to be one of the main focuses of my life.

I remained incarcerated until a little after I turned eighteen, about nine months. Meditation was helpful, but for the first couple of years I practiced only occasionally. I still thought that perhaps it was the drugs that had been the real problem. But after having stayed drug free and completely sober for almost two years, I came to the understanding that the causes of suffering in my life were rooted well below the surface manifestations of addiction.

I came to the realization that the only thing that had ever truly alleviated confusion and suffering in my life was meditation. So I began to explore the possibility of finding a spiritual solution to my living crisis. One of the foundational experiences of my early spiritual exploration was the twelve-step process of recovery from alcoholism and addiction. Although I had been sober for a couple of years and was attending twelve-step meetings regularly, I had never truly attempted to practice the principles of the steps, which together form a practical spiritual and psychological process. In 1990, I began to do what was suggested in the recovery program, which consisted of prayer, meditation, personal inventories, and amends.

Simultaneously, I began attending Buddhist meditation retreats and studying the ancient wisdom of the Eastern spiritual traditions. This was very helpful to me, because the twelve-step view of an externalized "higher power" had always proven difficult to accept. After a couple of years of shopping around in the spiritual supermarket of New Age American spiritual interpretations of the Buddhist, Hindu, and Sufi traditions of the East, and a short stint in a confused and corrupted cult, I came to find that the teachings of the Buddha, as originally taught (that is, pre–Mahayana Buddhism), were what resonated with me the most.

Over the past fifteen years I have been committed to studying and practicing the path of the Buddha. This practice has taken the form of numerous silent meditation retreats, ranging from a week to three months in length. It has also taken me, several times, to the monasteries of Southeast Asia and the pilgrimage sites of ancient India.

About ten years into my practice I began teaching meditation classes in the same juvenile hall in which I been incarcerated when I began this path. Having dropped out of school as a teenager, I also began studying at the local junior college and eventually moved on to earn a bachelor's degree and then a master's degree in counseling psychology.

In 2000, one of my teachers, Jack Kornfield, invited me to join a small group of Buddhist teachers to be trained over a four- or five-year period. That experience of mentorship, education, support, and encouragement proved to be transformative and became the foundation for expanding my ability to translate my personal spiritual experiences into the language and form of guiding others through the process of awakening. My practice and study under Jack, as well as others, connects me to an unbroken lineage of Buddhist practitioners that leads all the way back to Sid.

For the past few years I have been engaged in teaching, writing, and counseling. My aim is to use my early life's experiences to serve youth in juvenile halls, men in prison, and my generation on the streets and in society, and to do my best to make the teachings and practices of the Buddha accessible and available to all who are interested. In 2003 my memoir, *Dharma Punx,* was published. That book related my personal experience of how spiritual practice and service transformed my attitude and outlook on life.

This book is my offering to you of the path that I walk, the path of the spiritual revolutionary.

Noah Levine
NYC/LA/SF—2006

AGAINST THE STREAM

PART ONE

BASIC TRAINING

History and Fundamentals
of the Inner Revolution

The path of the spiritual revolutionary is a long-term and gradual journey toward awakening. If you are looking for a quick fix or easy salvation, turn back now, plug back into the matrix, and enjoy your delusional existence. This is a path for rebels, malcontents, and truth seekers. The wisdom and compassion of the Buddha is available to us all, but the journey to freedom is arduous. It will take a steadfast commitment to truth and, at times, counterinstinctual action.

You have at your disposal everything you need to undertake this journey. There is only one prerequisite: the willingness to do the work, to follow the path through the darkest recesses of your mind and heart, to stand up in the face of great resistance and fear and continue in the direction of freedom. For those who are willing, ability is a given.

The Buddha isn't a god or deity to be worshipped. He was a rebel and an overthrower, the destroyer of ignorance, the great physician who discovered the path to freedom from suffering. The Buddha left a legacy of truth for us to experience for ourselves. The practices and principles of his teachings lead to the direct experience of liberation. This is not a faith-based philosophy, but an experiential one. The point of the spiritual revolution is not to become a good Buddhist, but to become a wise and compassionate human being, to awaken from our life of complacency and ignorance and to be a buddha. In order to do so, it is helpful to study the life and teachings of the original rebel, Sid—the Buddha.

SID—THE REBEL SAINT

Let's go all the way back to the origin of this teaching and tradition—that is, to the Buddha, Siddhartha Gautama. How is it that we are still studying and practicing what he experienced and taught more than 2,500 years later and on the other side of the planet?

He was born by the name Siddhartha Gautama, but for the purposes of sacrilege and brevity I will refer to him as "Sid" until the point in the story when he wakes up—that is, the point at which he reaches enlightenment and becomes the Buddha.

Sid's father was the ruler of a small kingdom in northern India (now southern Nepal). Sid's mother, that ruler's first wife, died shortly after Sid's birth. His father then married his dead wife's sister, and Sid was raised by his father and his aunt.

There was a sage, probably a fortune-teller or astrologist, who came to the birth and said he'd had a vision: he had seen the coming of a future enlightened being. The sage foretold that this baby would grow into that being, and prophesied that he would become either a great enlightened spiritual master or a powerful warrior-king.

Sid's parents did not want their son to leave them and become a spiritual master, because spiritual masters do not hang out with their families much and rarely go into the family business. He was their only son and they wanted to keep him. They wanted him to inherit the family dynasty and become ruler. Fearing the truth of the sage's prediction, they kept him secluded. The family had three palaces, and he rarely had cause to leave them. Growing up in these palaces, he was surrounded by young, beautiful people all of the time. He never saw anyone who was old, sick, or dying. His parents were really trying to set it up so that he would have no reason to ask the big questions of life and seek answers through spiritual practice. If he thought life was perfect, there would be no reason for him to try to transcend it, right?

Their strategy seemed to work for quite a while. There was an exception, though: it is said that one time in his childhood when he was feeling a little uneasy he decided to chill out under a tree and watch his father, who was plowing a field or perhaps overseeing a groundbreaking ritual. Relaxing as he watched his father, he had a spontaneous experience of serenity. As a kid of only eight or nine, he had an overwhelming experience of peace. Though he went on with his adolescent years as before, he later recalled that experience of mindful relaxation, which I think is best described as an experience of total satisfaction—not needing or wanting anything to be different.

It is said that as a youth he was excellent at everything. Since his father was the king in a warrior caste and Sid was a prince, he was most likely a spoiled kid. There were periods in his young adult years when he was surrounded only by beautiful women; he was the only guy in his part of the palace. It is said that his life was one of access to constant pleasure. He reflected on this later, saying that during that time he sensed something was missing.

Though Sid's parents tried to keep their guard over him subtle, Sid eventually figured out that he was not allowed to leave the palaces on his own. He had everything he wanted in terms of physical needs, but he never got to explore the city without a retinue of guards and royal courtiers. What's more, while he was traveling from palace to palace or on the occasional procession through town, his father had guards clear the streets of anyone or anything that might be unpleasing to the eye. This included all of the elderly and sick.

By the time he was in his twenties, Sid had started to feel like a prisoner in his own home. One day he talked his attendant into sneaking him out of the palace. The two men slipped out and went into the nearby town. Walking for the first time in his life without a royal escort, Sid experienced what Buddhists call "the Four Messengers."

The first messenger was sickness and disease. For the first time in Sid's life, he saw people who were suffering from disease; because of his isolation, he had never seen illness before. Most of us grow up knowing about or experiencing some level of sickness and disease. It is a normal part of our lives. You can imagine how shocking it would be to see a sick person for the first time in your life as an adult. Sid asked his attendant if the debilitation he saw was going to happen to him as well, and the attendant replied that this is what happens to *all* humans.

We all eventually get sick or experience disease; it is the nature of the body.

The second messenger was a very old and frail person, the body deteriorating, skin sagging, and hair falling out. Sid asked his attendant what had happened, and his attendant replied that it was nothing more than what happens to *all* people. This was a shocking and powerful revelation to the overprotected Sid.

We all get old; this is the natural process of life.

The third messenger that they encountered was a corpse. Sid had never seen or heard of or even thought about death. He had been so sheltered that when he saw the dead body, he was horrified. (Keep in mind that this was before embalming or fancy caskets; this was a decomposing corpse by the side of the road.) Sid asked if that was going to happen to him and his family and demanded to know if there was any way to avoid it. He was told that death is inevitable. Not only that, he was informed, it happens over and over and over. Reincarnation, which was the popular perspective at that time, affirms that when one's body dies, the essence of the person is eventually reborn into another body. That is the cycle of birth and death.

Every body dies, but existence continues.

Sid was disconcerted to say the least, and perhaps more than a little pissed that all of this had been hidden from him for so long.

Then they saw the fourth messenger, a wandering spiritual seeker. Sid had never seen one of those before either, and he asked his attendant what the guy in the robes was doing. His attendant said that it was a sadhu—that is, someone who has dedicated his or her life to understanding the nature of life and death. A person in search of understanding reality. It was at that moment that Sid decided he knew what he had to do. As soon as Sid saw the spiritual seeker, he had a new sense of hope and faith that he would be able to come to a solution for this endless cycle of birth and death.

He vowed to overcome suffering and to awaken to the Truth.

If you are reading this book, I am guessing that you are searching for answers too. What was the first experience that made *you* think that the spiritual path was possible? For Sid it was seeing sickness, old age, and death, and then seeing a spiritual practitioner, but for each of us it will be a different experience that brought us to the path.

Anyway, Sid was recently married at the time of this revelation, and his wife had just given birth to a child. Theirs was an arranged marriage, and there may or may not have been any true love in it. Because his new spiritual resolve was stronger than his commitment to his family, he chose to leave his family and seek answers. He thought that since he and his family were only going to get sick and old and die, he had better go out and see if he could find a truth that would lead beyond sickness, old age, and death. He was motivated to find freedom not only for himself but for the benefit of his family and all beings in existence. His search was not a selfish one, as it might appear to some; it was an altruistic sacrifice for the good of all humanity.

Most people are initially confused and even troubled that he would leave his wife and child. I don't fully understand it myself. Imagine leaving your newborn child to go meditate, with no intention of returning until liberation was found! It turns out to be the right choice, however—and he does later return to his family, and his son also becomes a monk and gets enlightened. The search for truth may demand this kind of willingness and commitment, if not literally at least figuratively.

So Sid hit the streets. His attendant took him to the edge of town, but then Sid sent him away. Sid shaved his head, took off all his gold and fine clothing, put some rags around his body, and took off on foot with nothing but his desire to find freedom.

He sought out all of the spiritual masters of his time. He studied with several great Hindu masters and learned all of the practices and wisdom they had to offer. During the course of that instruction he had many very pleasant spiritual experiences.

What he was primarily taught during that phase was concentration practices like yoga and mantras—repetitive exercises of the body or mind that lead to one-pointedness. He was taught theories of existence that ranged from eternalism (existence forever) to nihilism (nonexistence after death).

Most of the concentration practices he experienced were subtle forms of aversion, allowing him to ignore pain and confusion but not changing his relationship to it. It is said that he had meditative experiences ranging from total bliss to complete nonexistence—experiences that took him to a level of understanding or peace—yet, when the concentration wore off he was still suffering, still subject to attachment to pleasure and aversion to pain, still identified with his physical body as his identity, still caught in the cycle of sickness, old age, and death.

Each one of the spiritual experiences that he had with those teachers taught him something new and wonderful that temporarily freed him. But as soon as he stopped doing a practice, the concentration wore off and he was left with ordinary consciousness. In other words, the practices did not transform his perspective. Because there was still fear, greed, and confusion in his heart, he knew that he had not reached full liberation.

Each teacher he studied with told Sid they had taught him all that they could, that he had accomplished what they thought to be spiritual liberation. Each of these teachers wanted Sid to be their spiritual heir, to stay and lead the community with them, but he had no interest in the power or prestige of being a guru. The practices he had learned did not lead him to total liberation, and he was not satisfied with the temporary spiritual experiences they offered. He decided to keep searching for the truth until he found complete freedom from the unsatisfactory nature of the cycle of rebirth. He vowed not to stop till he found a state of mind that wasn't dependent on any temporary meditative technique.

Sid's next bright idea was to break his identification with his body through self-mortification. He went off into the jungle and hooked up with a handful of other homeless homeys—aka sadhus—who were doing various practices to prove that they were not the body. They had the notion that if they denied their physical needs they could break the identification with the body, the physical form, and thereby reach the state of nonidentification and nonsuffering.

So they starved themselves, tortured their bodies, and tried to find freedom through extreme renunciation practices. It is said that Sid fasted for weeks on end. When he did eat, he consumed only morsels of rice or fruit each day. It was also popular, among these sadhus, to go without sleep and to spend days standing without ever sitting or lying down to rest. Sid wound up emaciated and close to physical death, but he was still suffering, still subject to attachment and aversion, still identified with his thoughts and feelings.

All told, Sid had spent seven years on the streets so far, following the conventional practices of his time and mastering the techniques offered in the Hindu tradition, including the more extreme techniques of the sadhus, and none of those practices had gotten him completely free. Now, close to starvation and still totally committed to waking up from the delusions of attachment, aversion, and identification that cause suffering, he reflected back on his childhood experience of being at peace beneath the tree. As he meditated on that experience, and on his ongoing battle against all forms of pleasure—a battle waged in the belief that attachment to pleasure is one of the delusions that cause identification with the body and lead to suffering and rebirth—Sid realized that neither pleasure nor comfort is the enemy. On the contrary, physical health and pleasure are wholesome experiences.

Sid had experienced both extremes of life, from gluttonous attachment to pleasure to radical rejection of all things pleasant, from aversion to discomfort to attachment to pain. Suddenly he could see that he needed to find some balance. So he left his homeys at the jungle squat and set off on his own to find the middle way. They accused him of selling out, saying he was giving up the true spiritual path. They knew he was going to eat and sleep and do all of the things that they had renounced. Hearing taunts of "food-eater" and all sorts of other insults, Sid stumbled to a nearby river and sat beneath a grove of trees, where he did sitting and walking meditation by himself.

A young girl from a nearby village saw him there, and realizing that he was close to dying of starvation, offered him the food she was taking home from the market. She returned to feed him yogurt and rice every day, and he gradually regained his health. Meanwhile, he spent his time in deep contemplation of the truth of the suffering and confusion that fuel the human cycle of dissatisfaction. He began to see that a key ingredient in his practice had been missing: it was simple *mind-fulness*. He began to practice an investigative present-time awareness, seeing the process of mind and body more and more clearly.

Once Sid had put a few pounds back on, he sat underneath a tree and vowed to stay there until he could see through the confusion in his mind. He was committed to not getting up from that seat until he had freed himself from all forms of mis-identification, attachment, and aversion—that is, until he never had to take birth again. Until he was totally free, he wasn't moving.

Can you imagine that kind of resolve?

So Sid sits there paying close attention to his mind and body, and he sits there and he sits there and he sits there, meditating on the causes of suffering and confusion. Feeling his breath as it comes and goes, investigating the pleasant unpleasant and neutral tone of each thought, feeling, and sensation. He opens his awareness in a more compassionate way, not trying to stop any experience no matter how unpleasant it may feel, but rather meeting each moment with love and kindness.

Many things happen to Sid that can be interpreted in retrospect as either internal or external experiences. A demonlike character named Mara shows up. Mara personifies all of the strong negative emotions that, when taken personally, cause us to suffer. These are the experiences of lust, fear, anger, and doubt, to name a few. Mara appears and tries to tempt the Buddha-to-be off his seat.

We can think of Mara as the aspect of mind often referred to as the ego, or perhaps the superego. Mara is afraid that Sid will see through the mind's illusion of control, and then Mara will not have power over him anymore. This Mara-mind will stop at nothing to sabotage Sid's (and our) resolve to be fully free from the attachment and aversion that cause suffering and dissatisfaction.

Mara's first line of attack is hatred, anger, and violence. Mara tries to expose Sid's attachment to pleasure by raining violence on him. Mara wages war on Sid, shooting arrows and throwing spears in an attempt to deter Sid from his goal. But Sid continues to sit. Seeing clearly that Mara is only an aspect of his mind, he radiates love and compassion throughout his being and turns the weapons of hatred into flowers that shower down all around him.

Next, Mara attacks with lust. A harem of beautiful women dancing naked arrive to tempt the Buddha-to-be with his desire. Sid continues to sit peacefully, reflecting on the fact that beneath the surface of temporary beauty is a bag of bones, flesh, and putrid fluids. He knows that the happiness he seeks will never come from a fleeting experience of sensual pleasure. He allows desire to arise and pass without clinging to it or identifying with it as personal. Feeling rejected and confused at Sid's refusal to accept their invitation of sexual pleasure, the dancing girls retreat.

Sid continues to sit there, unmoved by the mind's insistence. Mara takes one final stab at Sid, attacking with the most debilitating weapon in his arsenal: doubt. He challenges and taunts Sid with criticism and judgment. Mara tells Sid he is worthless and conceited to think he can fully awaken. Mara says, "Who do you think you are? Everyone is identified with the body, attached to pleasure, afraid of pain. How dare you try to be different?" Yet Sid has, by now, seen through his mind's limitations and has understood that by turning his awareness on the mind itself, he can see through the doubts and fears that arise. He knows that the doubts of the Mara-mind are not true; they are just another phenomenon that arises and passes. To prove his resolve, he touches the earth to bear witness to the four elements—earth, air, fire, and water—that make up all forms in existence, as he continues to be mindful and aware of his mind and body.

Mindfulness is the revolutionary insight that sets Buddhism apart from other traditions. Sid's main practice was investigative, compassionate, present-time awareness. Though Sid had learned to get the mind concentrated through his study with various gurus, he had not learned to open the consciousness to present-time awareness. It was this breakthrough that led to his freedom.

Around dawn, Mara understood that he no longer had any power over Sid. Mara had been defeated. With no more ammunition or means of attack, he sulked dejectedly off to find another victim. Sid just sat there feeling his breath and sensations coming and going, and he realized that everything is impermanent. Every physical and mental experience arises and passes. Everything in existence is endlessly arising out of causes and conditions. He saw that we all create suffering for ourselves through our resistance, through our desire to have things different than the way they are—that is, our clinging or aversion. Sid understood that if he just let go and was mindful and accepting without grabbing or pushing, he would be free and at peace with life.

He realized that when he really looked through the lens of concentration and then opened himself to mindful investigation, examining who was experiencing the moment and what the nature of his self was, he eventually could see that even the self is impermanent. He concluded that there is not a separate, solid self. Memory, consciousness, feeling, and perception exist, but there is not one solid, separate aspect that knows all of those experiences—that is, there is no independent entity or soul that remembers, is conscious, feels, or perceives. There are only memories, feelings, and perception. These are only experiences that are, as it were, experiencing themselves; there is not a separate, solid self experiencing them. Because there is memory, one remembers experiences; because of awareness one is aware of experiences—but in each case it is just awareness being aware of memory and experiences.

This battle with the Mara-mind and these three revolutionary insights brought about Sid's final transformation. He was no longer asleep; no longer subject to identification with greed, hatred, or delusion; no longer subject to rebirth. Sid was awake, the Buddha.

After the Buddha gained liberation under the Bodhi Tree— so called because he attained *bodhi,* or enlightenment, there— he said, in effect, What now? He was free. He had learned to accept pleasure as pleasure, pain as pain. He had seen through Mara's tricks and the ego's control and did not resist or attach to anything. He radiated care for the suffering in the world, but suffering no longer existed for the Buddha. So what now?

One important note: *Pain does still exist. Nirvana is not a state of constant pleasurable bliss. Suffering and pain are distinctly different. Many spiritual practitioners have the idea that if we are in pain we are doing something wrong and that spiritual practice, properly conducted, will make life pleasant all the time. According to*

Buddhist teachings, that was not the Buddha's experience. He went on to teach for forty-five years, and he had a bad back toward the end. His back hurt and he said so. That was the truth of that experience. He got injured and sick. He still had a human body, but he had no aversion, no attachment, and did not suffer because of his human body.

Even more important, the Buddha still had a human mind. Although he was free from the dictates of and misidentification with Mara as personal or powerful, Mara continued to visit the Buddha. Mara came back regularly to see if the wisdom and compassion of the Buddha had prevailed. Fear, desire, and doubt still arose in the enlightened Buddha's mind. The difference was that he responded every time with, "I see you, Mara." He did not take Mara's visitations personally and did not feel that he had to act on them; he saw fear, desire, and doubt as they were and did not react, but responded with care and understanding.

After attaining enlightenment, the Buddha was not sure what to do next. He spent many days continuing his meditation, reflecting on his newfound freedom and the path that had led him to deliverance from all forms of suffering and confusion. He reflected on the five factors that had led to his spiritual awakening and labeled them faith, effort, mindfulness, concentration, and wisdom (which encompassed compassion). The factor of mindfulness he broke down further still, into four distinct levels: body, feelings, mind, and the truth of experience. Then he formulated all of what he had learned and experienced into four universal truths consisting of twelve main factors, a formulation that later was referred to—and still generally is referred to—as the four noble truths and the eight-fold path. We'll take a look at these teachings in a bit.

With the path of awakening fully understood and comprehended, the Buddha considered sharing his insights with others, but he was hesitant because his revolutionary insights were so contrary to the common teachings and views of his time. He was pretty sure they would not be understood or accepted by the masses, because they are so subtle, so simple, and so contrary to the natural human instinct. To ask people to accept pain and a spiritual liberation that does not include bliss all of the time seemed crazy. He was unsure if people would be willing to do the work necessary to free themselves from attachment to and craving for pleasure.

Buddhism is often referred to as an atheistic tradition, but that isn't an accurate description. The Buddha acknowledged the existence of celestial beings or gods, and in fact he later recounted that a god named Brahma came to him and implored him to teach. Perhaps God, like Mara (who could be seen as the devil), is just another aspect of our minds, God being the wise aspect and Mara being the unwise aspect.

It would be more true to say that real Buddhism is *non*theistic. While the Buddha acknowledged gods, he concluded that they did not have the power to free us from suffering, and thus they were not part of his formulation. They were the beneficiaries, though: the Buddha is often called the teacher of humans *and gods,* because the gods are suffering as well and the Buddha can and did teach the gods the path to freedom.

The god Brahma saw that the Buddha was hesitant to teach the Dharma—the truth of his enlightenment—and implored the Buddha to reconsider. There are some who will understand this teaching, Brahma explained. The Buddha replied that it

was a freedom that was very difficult to attain. He character-
ized it as being counterinstinctual to human beings: the natural
human instinct is to resist, avoid, or meet with aversion all
things that are unpleasant, and to grasp at, hold on to, and
crave all things that are pleasurable. He explained that his
experience along the whole spiritual path was one that went
"against the stream" of ordinary human consciousness.

The Buddha felt that the masses would never be willing to
practice the kind of renunciation, mindfulness, concentration,
and morality that it takes to become free. Brahma agreed with
the Buddha, but he insisted that there would be some in every
generation that were not completely asleep, that had only a
little dust in their eyes. The Dharma, as experienced and
taught by the Buddha, Brahma insisted, could clear away that
dust and allow those who chose to undertake this training to
awaken.

The Buddha reflected on Brahma's plea as he was sitting
next to a lotus pond. He saw that most of the lotus plants
stayed stuck in the mud, beneath the surface and the light of
day, and some were barely breaking the surface, but there
were a few lotuses that had broken forth into the sunlight and
blossomed. The Buddha likened humans to the lotus flowers.
Out of the deluded mud of human existence, filled with greed,
hatred, and delusion, in a world where wars, oppression, and
lust rule the masses, there are those who can and will rise
above the muck and emerge victorious against suffering.

Being convinced that it would be a worthy endeavor to start
a spiritual revolution, the Buddha decided that he must offer
the path to freedom to all who cared to follow it. He thought

of his homeless homeys he had been practicing with in the forest and thought that if anyone could understand this radical teaching it was them. So the Buddha set forth to teach the Dharma.

THE FOUR NOBLE TRUTHS OF THE REVOLUTIONARY PATH TO FREEDOM

The first teachings the Buddha gave after his enlightenment were the four noble truths. These were first delivered to the same ascetics he had been practicing with in the forest before his awakening. This giving of the truths is often referred to as the setting in motion of the wheel of Dharma. The term *wheel* is used because the Buddha's teachings explain the *cycle* or *circle* of existence. Furthering that imagery, the wheel of Dharma consists of eight trainings, the eightfold path, which are seen as the wheel's spokes. When a wheel is set in motion it revolves. One could say that all of Buddhism revolves around these central teachings, because every Buddhist tradition includes some form of the four noble truths and the eightfold path. So with this turning of the wheel, the Buddha started a revolution that continues to this day.

When the Buddha first returned to his old pals, the homeless homeys, they were hesitant to listen to what he had to say. They shunned him as a food-eater and sellout. But the Buddha's newfound freedom and happiness were so apparent and attractive that they couldn't help but listen to what he had to say.

The First Truth

The Buddha taught that life by its very nature is unsatisfactory, that some level of difficulty exists for all unenlightened beings in creation. We face sickness, old age, and death; the sense pleasures we do experience don't last; and physical and perhaps emotional pain is a given in life.

There are two levels to this truth. The first is the pain of existence that we can't do anything about. The second is the suffering and unhappiness that we create for ourselves due to our lack of wisdom and our vain attempts to control the uncontrollable—that is, the transient nature of all physical, emotional, and mental phenomena. We are born into a realm of constant change. Everything is decaying. We are continually losing all that we come into contact with. Our tendency to get attached to impermanent experiences causes sorrow, lamentation, and grief, because eventually we are separated from everything and everyone that we love. Our lack of acceptance and understanding of this fact makes life unsatisfactory.

Pain and suffering are two completely different experiences. Pain is unavoidable. Suffering is self-created.

Some level of dissatisfaction exists for all unenlightened beings.

For some this is a revelation, a normalizing statement that brings about a great sense of relief. Finally we are being told the truth: life isn't always easy and pleasant. We already know this to be true, but somehow we tend to go through life thinking that there is something wrong with us when we experience sadness, grief, and physical and emotional pain. The first truth points out that this is just the way it is. There is nothing wrong with you: you have just been born into a realm where pain is a given.

The Second Truth

There is a cause for all this dissatisfaction and suffering. It is our craving for life to be filled exclusively with pleasure. That craving for pleasure creates a natural reaction of aversion to the pains and difficulties of life. This truth can be seen as a simple lack of acceptance: unwilling to accept the pleasures and pains as they are, we go about clinging to the experiences we like and trying to get rid of the ones we don't like.

We also create suffering for ourselves due to our craving to exist permanently—that is, our craving for eternal pleasure. When life is good, we want it to go on forever. At other times, though, we create suffering for ourselves through our craving to not exist at all—the craving for nonexistence, which results from the desire to escape from the pains and difficulties of life. All suicidal tendencies can be understood in the light of this desire to escape suffering. When life is very difficult or painful, we want to no longer exist.

As long as greed, hatred, and delusion exist within our hearts, suffering will continue in our lives, no matter how much we seek to experience pleasure and avoid pain.

Craving is the problem. Desires are natural, but craving—which is painful—is the extreme aspect of desire.

The Third Truth

Freedom from suffering is possible. There is a way to relate to all experience that is in harmony with the reality of constant change and the ultimately impersonal nature of all things. When greed, hatred, and delusion are destroyed, a state of peace and happiness is all that remains. This is the state of freedom from suffering referred to as Nirvana (which means *cessation*).

The Buddha experienced it, and if he could do it through his own efforts, others can too.

We all have mini-experiences of this—moments in our life, perhaps even on a daily basis, when we are free from greed, hatred, and delusion, when we are satisfied and at peace. Yet we tend to ignore or forget those experiences. The truth of craving blocks the truth of freedom. The path of rebellion, the Buddha's path, will bring us to a more consistent state of freedom.

Freedom is available in this lifetime.

The Fourth Truth

The path to freedom consists of eight factors (often referred to as the eightfold path). These eight important areas of comprehension and practice, which make up the spiritual revolutionary's training manual, can be broken down into three sections:

Wisdom
    1. Understanding
    2. Intention

Conduct
    3. Speech
    4. Action
    5. Livelihood

Meditation
>   6. Effort
>   7. Mindfulness
>   8. Concentration

Studying and contemplating these eight factors, the enlightened revolutionary can experience the freedom celebrated and taught by the Buddha.

THE EIGHTFOLD PATH

The factors of the eightfold path—factors regarding wisdom, conduct, and meditation—are not linear, nor are they meant to be taken one at a time. They are all developed simultaneously, and each factor has correlations with and is a support for other factors. Trainings for each of these factors, trainings in mind and body, can be taken up simultaneously. The revolutionary can and should begin meditating and being careful with his or her actions from the very beginning; however, for the sake of explaining the path, I will take the factors one at a time in the order that they are listed above, broken down into the three categories of wisdom, conduct, and meditation.

Wisdom

Like all good trainings, this path begins with theory and then moves on to practical exercises. The first two factors, *understanding* and *intention,* deal with wisdom. The would-be revolutionary should strive to understand the awakened, enlightened view of existence and the importance of having the correct aims and thoughts about what will bring about the spiritual revolution of freedom and happiness. The awakened view is the understanding that all things are impermanent, ultimately impersonal, and on some level unsatisfactory. I experience this in my relationship to my material possessions, like my car or motorcycle. I know that my vehicles are temporary, that they don't bring lasting happiness, and that eventually I will be separated from them. Because I understand all of this, I can enjoy my toys without clinging to them or suffering when they break down. Let's look at the two aspects of wisdom in a bit more detail.

1. *Right understanding* is knowing the truth of the way we create suffering for ourselves due to our craving for pleasure and our constant, vain attempts to escape from pain. The concepts of *karma, reincarnation,* and *impermanence* are central to the factor of understanding.

When we pay attention to life, it is easy to recognize that every action has a consequence: when we cling, we suffer; when we act selfishly or violently, we cause suffering for ourselves or others. This is the teaching of karma: positive actions have positive outcomes; negative actions have negative outcomes.

Negative actions include intentionally killing any living being, stealing, participating in sexual misconduct, lying, using harsh or abusive language, gossiping, and practicing envy, covetousness, or ill will.

Positive actions include abstaining from all of the above and practicing such things as kindness, compassion, generosity, forgiveness, and understanding.

Within the Buddhist worldview, karma is always taught within a multilife schema—that is, the outcome of one's actions can come into fruition in this lifetime or another. Reincarnation is the truth of continued existence from life to life. It is not our personality or soul that is reborn, but our karma. It is our accumulated positive and negative actions that continue. From this perspective, we are experiencing in the present a reverberation from choices we made in the past. Likewise, our future experiences will be colored by the choices we make in the present.

Next we must understand that all things are subject to change, without a permanent self. We tend to take our *selves* to be our *egos,* or what some like to call our *souls*. But the truth is that there is no solid separate or permanent self. The self itself is impermanent. Even in rebirth it is not the self that is reborn, but the karmic momentum.

The teachings of karma and reincarnation may seem too mystical or daunting to easily understand and accept. But that is the beauty of Buddhism: you don't have to accept it or understand it; rather, people are encouraged to investigate it thoroughly and find out for themselves if it is true or not. We may never be able to fully grasp the root causes and conditions of our past karmic momentum, which has brought us to where we find ourselves in this life, but if we look closely we can see the truth of cause and effect in our day-to-day life. The more we meditate, the clearer this will all become.

Karma, reincarnation, and impermanence all merge in the Buddhist concept of the *dependent origination* of all things, a concept that says everything is unfolding based on causes and conditions. Our happiness or suffering is dependent on how we relate to the present moment. If we cling now, we suffer later. If we let go and respond with compassion or friendliness, we create happiness and well-being for the future.

Dependent origination begins with ignorance or confusion and ends with suffering. It is the map of how we create suffering, but it is also the path to avoiding suffering. There are twelve links in the cycle of cause and effect, and these links explain how we create and relate to karma.

We are all born into a state of ignorance. We learn how to respond to experience through internal and external conditioning and karmic momentum. At some point, we all realize that neither our instinctual nor our learned reactions are bringing about true happiness or freedom. This teaching involves both the way karma works from moment to moment and the way it works in reincarnation—that is, from life to life. For the sake of staying practical in the form of mind training and liberation, I will stick to the present-time-awareness view.

This is the technical version of dependent origination, with the components listed in order from one to twelve.

1. Ignorance, which leads to

2. Mental formations (thoughts or emotions), which lead to

3. Consciousness, which requires

4. Material form, which has

5. Six senses (physical sensation, hearing, seeing, smelling, tasting, and mental thoughts) through which stimuli generate

6. Contact, which creates sense impressions that generate

7. Feelings (pleasant, unpleasant, or neutral) that generate

8. Craving (either to keep or to get rid of the feeling), which causes

9. Grasping (or aversion), which generates

10. Becoming (identifying with the experience as personal), which generates

11. Birth (incarnating around the grasping), which generates

12. Suffering or dissatisfaction

Let's look at an example of that sequence in action:

1. I am walking down the street, not paying attention. *(Ignorance)*

2. I see an ice-cream shop, and the thought arises, "Ice cream is delicious and it makes me happy." *(Mental formation)*

3. I decide that I will have some ice cream. *(Consciousness)*

4. I walk into the ice-cream shop. *(Material form, my body)*

5. Inside the shop, I see and smell the ice cream and I begin to think about what kind I shall order. *(Senses)*

6. The ice cream smells sweet and creamy. *(Contact)*

7. I enjoy the smells of the waffle cones and hot fudge. *(Feelings, pleasant)*

8. I decide that I need a triple-scoop hot-fudge sundae in an extra-large waffle cone. *(Craving)*

9. After a few bites I am full, but I continue to eat the

whole thing because it tastes so good. *(Grasping at pleasure)*

10. I wish I hadn't eaten the whole thing, or had any ice cream at all. I think I was stupid for eating it. *(Becoming)*

11. I blame myself for being so gluttonous. *(Birth)*

12. I feel physically sick and emotionally drained. *(Suffering)*

Dependent origination is the downstream current of life. Without intentional mind training we just float along, addicted to our habitual reaction. We float downstream from ignorance, to consciousness, to identification with the sensation. Then the desire for more or less of the experience arises. And we continue to be drawn downstream, from the indulgence of it, to the identification with it, to taking birth as the sensation and then it passes away. Because of impermanence, it dies. Then we follow the same progression over and over. This process happens many times each minute. There is contact and sensation over and over.

The mindfulness that Buddhism encourages allows us to respond in the moment of contact with pleasure or pain in a more skillful way. When we are paying attention to our inner experience at the moment of awareness of the feeling (whether the feeling is pleasant, unpleasant, or neutral), we can break the cycle of habitually reacting out of attachment or aversion. It is at this moment of awareness, at the link between contact and craving, that we have the ability to choose to let go and head in the direction of happiness or hold on and continue to suffer.

My friend and colleague Vinny Ferraro likes to refer to our practice here as "letting each moment die its own natural death." Attachment and aversion are attempts to resuscitate or kill an experience. Mindfulness allows us to receive the experience directly and respond more like a compassionate hospice worker than an aggressive ER doctor.

What is most important, and the greatest weapon of the spiritual revolutionary, is how we meet each moment within ourselves. The mind trained in investigative awareness has the ability to break this cycle, has the free will to bring mindfulness to each moment at which desire becomes indulgence, at which feeling becomes craving.

From the perspective of Buddhist psychology, this is the only place we *do* have free will. If we don't bring mindfulness to the experience of contact becoming feeling, or desire becoming indulgence, we are slaves to that sensation and to our karma, our past tendencies. We will stay in this cycle forever unless we train ourselves to bring attention to it and let go of the grasping and identification that cause suffering.

Most of us are unable to break this pattern without a serious amount of effort, training, and dedication to being free from it. We go through our whole lives getting pushed along by our karma, our childhood conditioning, or the momentum that we brought into this incarnation from a past one. Without training our attention to be in the present, we cannot actually control our reactions. From this perspective there is no free will without paying close attention.

Basically, this first factor in the eightfold path shows us that we can choose to purify our actions and therefore experience happiness and freedom from suffering, or we can continue to ignore the facts and endlessly wander from experience to experience and life to life covered in confusion. Only if we understand the path to freedom, karma, and truths of impermanence, not-self, and dissatisfaction can we find our way out of the maze of confusion and truly understand reality.

2. *Right intentions* are the goals or aims of our actions. They are the reasons behind our actions.

Having learned the theoretical truths of existence, we must then align our thoughts and intentions toward the goal of freedom. This consists of redirecting our thoughts and intentions from the negative karma–producing thoughts such as lust, ill will, and cruelty to the positive intentions of kindness, compassion, generosity, forgiveness, and understanding.

In order to find freedom we must aim our life's energy and actions toward being free from ill will, aversion, and wishing harm on ourselves and others. We must also be free from the lust for pleasure, which is clearly the cause of much confusion in our world. Lust is desire that is out of control. Our intention doesn't need to be free from desire itself, but only free from the extreme of craving. *Wanting* something is not a problem, but *having to have* something is—it's a setup for disappointment.

Intention plays a central role in the spiritual life. It is that from which volitional actions come—the actions that are at the heart of karma, which literally means *action*. Most of us have a misunderstanding of karma: we think that it refers to the result. Something bad happens and we say, "That was my karma" or "That was her karma." Actually, karma is action itself. The result is the karmic fruit. And that karmic fruit—the outcome of an action—comes from our intention, not the act itself. For instance, if we accidentally kill an insect by walking down the street, there is no negative karma created because it was not our intention to kill. But when we volitionally kill insects because we are afraid of them or because we hate them, we are committing an intentional act that does bear a negative consequence or fruit.

This is an important distinction: karmic results come from our positive or negative intentions, not from the actions themselves. From this perspective a person can even harm or take human life accidentally—that is, without negative intention—and not have karmic repercussions.

There are two levels of intention. The first is simply having the correct intention. This means training our mind in thoughts that are free from craving and ill will. It means thinking about the welfare of all beings, including oneself. This sort of intention may be as simple as paying attention to our motives and abstaining from actions that are motivated by greed, hatred, or delusion. For example, when we are angry and lashing out at someone, that is obviously an aversive reaction, an intentionally harmful act.

The second level of intention goes beyond just being free from negative thoughts to also intentionally cultivating positive thoughts. This is referred to as the supermundane level, or spiritual thought. Here we begin to cultivate thoughts of loving-kindness, compassion, and forgiveness. We attempt to use our mental faculties to think about, to consider, to reason, to reflect, and to apply spiritual principles. We intentionally train our minds to think thoughts that are focused on spiritual matters rather than material ones. This higher level of thought is the proper use of intentional thinking. Most of the time our minds are filled with planning how to get our next fix of pleasure or, at the least, how to avoid pain or failure. On this higher level of spiritual thought, we are intentionally thinking about generosity and compassion.

The first, mundane, level of intention involves practicing nonharming. It is simply damage control. The second, supermundane, level involves intentionally using our minds to get free from suffering and dissatisfaction. In this higher aspect of intention, we use our minds—we in fact *train* our minds—in the practice of meditation, reflecting on impermanence and on how craving and grasping create suffering.

As we observe the way our minds and bodies react to pleasure and pain, we begin to clearly understand how ultimately impersonal this human experience is, and how through our delusions and self-centeredness we are constantly making it personal and taking it personally. We are constantly identifying with the experience that is unfolding right now. We tend to feel that all of our thoughts are *me, my, mine,* when the truth is that everything is just the experience of the mind. It is not "*my* mind"; it is "*the* mind"—an ultimately impersonal experience of *a* mind. There is consciousness experiencing thoughts, but it is not *our* consciousness. We don't own that consciousness, and it's not even permanent. It's just consciousness, arising and passing as do all things.

Here's another way to put it. We are not the mind or its contents, nor are we even the experiencer of the mind. The mind experiences itself.

So our practice is to overcome identification with negative thoughts through renunciation. When we let go of or renounce ill will and the satisfying of lust, we cut off suffering at its root causes. Renunciation is not about pushing something away; it is about letting go. It's facing the fact that certain things cause us pain, and they cause other people pain. Renunciation is a commitment to let go of the things that create suffering. It is the intention to stop hurting ourselves and others.

For example, when I realized that my craving for pleasure and my hatred of pain had become addiction to drugs and alcohol, I had to renounce all forms of participation in intoxication. Through letting go of drugs and booze, I was left with the raw emotions and fears that had been fueling the addictions. But by facing the aversion to those emotions and the craving for the insensibility of intoxication, I came to understand that the craving and addition were all in my mind, and that I had the ability to choose, one moment at a time, not to run away from pain by drowning it in false pleasure. Eventually it became clear that, as the Buddha taught, pain was not the enemy, but just another given aspect of life.

It's similar to fire. Ill will, cruelty, and craving all burn, and in their extreme forms they consume us. They are natural phenomena, however, and if we have a wise relationship to the mind, they are not a problem at all. Thus it is not about pushing these thoughts and feelings away or pretending we don't experience them. It is about training the mind to not pick up the fire and therefore not get burned. That is renunciation. We have the choice to no longer stick our hands in the flames.

Easier said than done, but possible nonetheless.

Having a positive intention is a protection against suffering. Just about every day at his home in Dharamsala in northern India, His Holiness the Dalai Lama, the exiled leader of Tibet, receives hundreds of Tibetan refugees. They tell him the most gruesome stories of how they were raped and tortured by the Communist Chinese and then walked across the Himalayas to reach him. In many cases some of their relatives died along the way, and most had to leave loved ones behind. Their stories tell of tremendous suffering. The Dalai Lama hears these stories one after another. An interviewer once asked him, "How can you listen to all of this suffering without it tearing you apart? How do you sit with all this tremendous suffering, being exiled from your own country, and the genocide of the people that you are supposed to be the leader of?" He answered, "My sincere motivation is my protection." His sincere intention to respond with compassion and understanding to the suffering that he hears about sustains him. He sees beyond Communist China's occupation of his country; he also sees the suffering of the oppressors. Because the Dalai Lama fully understands karma, he knows that the Communist Chinese too are creating suffering for themselves in the present and future. The intention to meet all suffering with compassion is his refuge.

It would be quite easy for the Dalai Lama to react with anger and hatred to the Communist Chinese. Instead, choosing the radical approach of the spiritual revolutionary, he responds with compassion, kindness, and understanding. He refers to the Chinese as "my friends, the enemy."

Through letting go of ill will, we also realize that acting out our hatred only causes more hatred. Picking up the burning ember of ill will from the fire to throw at our enemy burns us before it burns them.

Perhaps most important, we must relax and realize that the stance of the spiritual revolutionary comes with time, when we have learned to cultivate the right intention. This perspective begins to unfold with practice. Simply thinking about it isn't enough; we must practice it. This redirection of our intention comes more alive when we develop the moral and ethical practices of nonharming that follow in the next section. With the gathering of the attention in the formal practice of meditation, our mind gets concentrated and our awareness penetrates the truth of what is happening in the here and now. We directly experience the impermanent and dissatisfactory nature of our negative thoughts and we begin to see that they are not as personal as we thought.

You'll remember that understanding and intention compose wisdom, the first level of the eightfold path. The Buddha said that trying to comprehend right understanding and right intention without ethical conduct and the training of meditation, the final two levels of the path, is like trying to row a boat across a river without untying it from the dock. He went on to say it was like trying to row upstream without any oars. Those who try will just get swept away by their confusion, ill will, and self-serving intentions based on greed and hatred.

This brings us to the second section of the training: conduct.

Conduct

Ethical conduct is based on an intention of nonharming and compassion toward all in speech, action, and livelihood. We will look at those three elements in turn.

3. *Right speech* entails the nonharmful use of communication. Having firmly established the correct view, understand-

ing, thought, and intention about the path to freedom, spiritual revolutionaries must then align their actions with these intentions. This begins with realizing the power of communication to cause harm or to bring about positive change and happiness.

With the right intention comes the willingness to abstain from speaking harmful words. The Buddha classified speech that is harsh, malicious, vain, untrue, or gossipy as being a harmful misuse of communication. Being wise and careful about what we say, write, and otherwise communicate will bring more well-being to ourselves and to all those with whom we come into contact.

A good basic guideline for our speech is to reflect on whether what we are saying is both true and useful. There may be times when we are honest in what we say, but our words are too brutal or harsh. And there may be other times when we are deliberately being kind with the words we choose, but what we are saying is not totally true.

Most of us know the consequence of dishonesty. When we lie, we live in fear of being caught. I spent much of my early life making up stories about who I was and where I came from. Those lies built on each other until I didn't know what I had told to whom. When I came to the path of Dharma, it took me time and much intentional practice to learn to be rigorously honest with myself and others.

Harsh speech has been my habit since an early age. I have always loved the shock value of swearing. Over the years my vocabulary hasn't changed much, but my intentions have changed a lot. I still swear quite a bit, but now my use of *fuck, shit, bitch,* and *balls* serves more as an exclamation point to illustrate my sentiment than a sword to cause harm with. It is my feeling that swearing isn't always harsh or malicious. Like everything else, it depends on our intention—in this case, our intention in using the language.

Likewise with gossip, there is a difference between talking about someone who isn't present with the intention to cause harm or with the intention to share concern. Most of us have felt the effects of the "he said, she said" game. When I look at my intentions behind gossiping, I often realize that I am seeking power through sharing information. This is not a useful form of communication. Now, though I still often get caught up in it, I am aware of the negative consequences it may have. A wise friend once told me that anything people say when I am not present is none of my business. That piece of advice has saved me from a lot of suffering.

The Buddha spoke of the inevitability of praise and blame, fame and disrepute, pleasure and pain, gain and loss. For the topic of speech, it is important to accept that while some will offer praise, others will place blame.

Practicing speech that is true and useful is the intention of the rebel forces.

4. *Right action* is equally important. The real revolutionary is committed to nonviolence. The Buddha's radical stance of nonviolence is a wise and practical path to personal and societal change. When we commit to waking up and revolting against the ignorance and oppression of classism, racism, sexism, and all forms of greed, hatred, and delusion in this world, the first step we must take in that revolt is a personal dedication to purify our actions from these things that cause

harm. The minimum commitment necessary for the path toward enlightenment and freedom is renunciation of taking life, of dishonesty, and of sexual misconduct.

Mindfulness is a must if we want to be aware of and present with the emotions that provoke harmful actions. First and foremost, an awareness of our inner experience—which includes thoughts, feelings, preferences, emotions, conditioning, and sensations—requires a mind that is free from the obscuring effects of intoxicants. Mind- and mood-altering drugs such as alcohol, marijuana, narcotics, barbiturates, and hallucinogens cloud the mind and lead to an inability to be fully present for the inner experience. The Buddha was clear that the spiritual revolution requires a sober and drug-free mind. (This restriction would not apply to the prescribed psychotropic medications that some people need in order to function skillfully in the world.)

From the foundation of an unintoxicated mind, we can then train ourselves to respond to anger with compassionate investigation, respond to greed with acceptance and humility, and commit to nonharming on every level of existence. This includes letting go of all forms of dishonesty—that is, stealing, lying, and cheating. It also includes acknowledging the harm that is often caused through unwise and unskillful use of sexual energy and making a sincere commitment to a wise and careful relationship to sexuality. Traditionally this means abstaining from all sexual relations that we know will be the cause of harm to oneself or another. (More about sex in a later section.)

Wise and careful action, from a foundation of sober awareness, is the way of the revolutionary.

5. *Right livelihood* means choosing a profession that is not involved in harming the world. Because we spend so much of our lives working, it is incredibly important that we find a way of making a living that does not add to the confusion and suffering in the world. Our livelihood also impacts karma: since all intentional actions have reciprocal outcomes, the time we spend on the job is a major generator of karma. It doesn't work to practice spiritual principles at home while earning a living through something that creates harm in the world. By participating in a harm-causing career, we not only hurt other beings or our world, we create future harm for ourselves. Some of the traditional jobs to avoid are killing living beings, selling weapons, selling intoxicants, and making money in the sex industry. All of these jobs create suffering and confusion on some level. So even if the easiest way we find to make money is through selling booze or drugs, we need to choose different work. If we profit from substances that cause confusion and suffering, we are actually committing an act of self-sabotage. If our job is, say, bartending, close attention to our intention may reveal that our work is motivated by greed. A bartender witnesses the suffering of alcoholism and the confusion of drunkenness, yet profits from that suffering. Because profiting from the suffering and confusion of others has a negative karmic consequence, those who wish to be free from suffering should avoid all such jobs.

Working in the sex industry as a stripper, prostitute, or purveyor of Internet porn is perhaps a more subtle form of wrong livelihood. Sexuality is natural and sex for sale is an ancient profession, but, again, if we look deeply, it is not hard to see that the lust that motivates such an industry has negative

effects on both the workers and the customers.
least, participation in the sex industry is depend
on lust and attachment, the very causes of suffering and dis
satisfaction for people.

Spiritual revolutionaries must be committed not to what is
easiest but to what is most beneficial to themselves and the
world. Remember: we have set our intentions to go against the
stream. It is not the easiest way, to be sure, but it is perhaps
the only way to achieve freedom and bring about positive
change.

Meditation

Once we are committed to nonharming conduct in speech,
action, and livelihood, we can benefit more easily from the
meditative trainings of mindfulness and concentration. Effort
underlies these other aspects of meditation, as it does *all* of the
factors on the path.

6. *Right effort* is the intentional application of energy. Everything we have talked about so far takes effort. None of these
practices or principles are easy to develop. Going against the
stream is an act of intentional defiance and redirection of our
life's energy. We all have the energy necessary for this inner
and outer revolution, but only with wise and intentional use of
that energy—that is, with *effort*—can we master Buddhism's
liberating practices and avoid the habitual reactive tendencies
that create more attachment and suffering in our lives.

Some of the ways we must use our energy and effort
include avoiding the things that create suffering, replacing
harmful thoughts and actions with thoughts and actions that

create well-being and peace, developing wisdom and compassion through meditation and wise actions, and sustaining the wisdom and compassion that arise through careful attention.

When it comes to training our minds and hearts in the path of freedom, each practitioner must find the balance of applying the right amount of effort: not so much that we get strained, not so little that we get spaced out. Developing a balanced effort and energy in our spiritual life is key to the revolution.

The image of the stream works well for the implied effort that it takes to awaken and overthrow ignorance. In the beginning we are all floating downstream. At some point we become aware that the currents are dragging us down and that we are no longer satisfied with the status quo of human existence. We realize that life is passing us by and that true happiness is not going to be found by merely floating downstream. So we turn to spiritual practices as a tool to find the satisfaction that has been eluding us. Meditation and spiritual principles give us the tools to start going against the stream. In the early days and months of practice it can be a struggle simply to stop floating down the stream in the old habitual way. As we bring awareness to our habits, tendencies, and worldviews, we at first may see only how confused we have been. The more we pay attention, the clearer it will become how radical a path we have undertaken. And although we long for quick progress, we can achieve nothing until we stop the downward spiral.

Even that takes a lot of effort. There we are, flailing away in the middle of the stream, and we're doing nothing but trying to stop going downstream with the current. Then we're stopped, but that's all; we haven't begun to make progress in the other direction yet, because we're in the center of the stream, trying to swim against the current. If we put too much effort into it, we feel tired out and overwhelmed, and it's easy to give up and simply float downstream again. We have to find a balance of effort that is sustainable. The path of the spiritual revolutionary is a long-term endeavor. It is more like a marathon than a quarter-mile sprint.

The skillful way of practice is not to force yourself to the center of the stream with an overexuberant effort. As anyone who has ever tried to swim upstream in a river with a strong current knows, to get anywhere you have to swim from side to side. You can't go straight up the center of the current; you have to swim diagonally toward one side, then across toward the other, to make any progress. This requires a balance between effort and relaxation. Only a steady and relaxed effort will carry you upstream, against the current. It's that kind of steady and sustainable effort that allows us to make progress on the path of both inner and outer rebellion.

The Buddha likened spiritual effort to the tuning of a stringed instrument. If the strings are too tight, it doesn't play correctly. If the strings are too loose, it doesn't sound right either.

The path to freedom takes great effort and fine-tuning.

7. *Mindfulness,* or present-time awareness, is essential to finding our way on the eightfold path. In fact, all of the other factors of the path depend on mindfulness of the present moment. Present-time awareness is the experience of knowing what is happening as it happens. The revolution is dependent on the rebel forces being present in mind as well as in body. That is the only way to overthrow the oppression of greed, hatred, and delusion.

This sort of awareness takes intentional training of the mind. Our attention is naturally scattered, the mind constantly swinging from present, to future, to past, to fantasy. Even for those who know that present-time awareness is the key to freedom, getting the attention to stay in the present is an extremely difficult practice. To be mindful of the present-time experiences of thoughts, feeling, sensations, and actions, we must vigilantly and continually redirect the attention to the here and now.

The formal training of mindfulness takes place on the meditation cushion, through redirecting the attention or awareness to the breath, body, feeling tone, and process of mind, as well as the state of mind that has arisen. Yet life demands more than just paying attention during formal meditation periods. We must have the intention to be mindful and aware during *all* aspects of life.

The body is the best place to start. Through redirecting the attention from the thinking mind to the felt sense of the body, we begin to condition the attention to be in the here and now. This is done by returning our attention to the physical experience each time it wanders into thinking about the past or future. The practice of mindfulness of the breath is especially helpful at the outset, because we are always breathing. Given that the breath is always happening in the present moment, we know that if we are aware of the sensations of the breath, we have successfully brought the attention into the present moment. This first level of mindfulness offers us an experience of relaxation and letting go of the insistent wandering of the thinking aspect of our mind.

(The appendix contains instructions for various meditative trainings. For help with this first level of mindfulness, see two of those trainings: Mindfulness of Breathing and Mindfulness of the Breath and Body.)

The breath and the body are only the beginning of the mindfulness practice. Once we have established some level of present-time awareness and attention to the physical sensations of the body, we undertake training to bring attention to the feeling tone of the particular experience we are paying attention to.

Every single experience has a feeling tone to it—a quality of pleasantness, unpleasantness, or neutrality that we can perceive when we are mindful. An awareness of the experience and its pleasant or unpleasant tone is essential if we are to progress on the path to freedom. Our habitual reaction to pleasurable experiences is to cling to them, while our habitual reaction to unpleasant experiences is to resist or push them away. Clinging and aversion are the cause of most of the suffering we create for ourselves, and the subtle roots of all greed and hatred.

This second level of mindfulness, then, offers us awareness of the causes of suffering. Through being mindful of the experience and its feeling tone, we can directly examine our inner relationship of clinging to pleasure and aversion to discomfort, and we can react deliberately, choosing to let go at the root or cause of suffering. Without intentional mindfulness at this level of experience, we have no choice but to stay stuck in the habits of aversion and clinging, and as a result we float with the current on the stream of unenlightened existence. In other words, paying careful attention to the present moment and our inner relationship to the tone of experience allows us to rebel against the conditioned patterns by simply meeting the unpleasant, the neutral, and the pleasant with acceptance and understanding. A simple choice is at the heart of that rebellion: we can either stay asleep (clinging and avoiding) and continue to suffer, or we can wake up (practicing mindfulness and letting go) and find a deeper sense of well-being and happiness.

(See Mindfulness of the Feeling Tone instructions in the appendix.)

The third level of mindfulness brings attention to the process and contents of our mind. Having established present-time awareness of the body and feeling tone of experience, we then turn our mindfulness to the mind itself. This is done through paying close attention to our states of mind as they arise, including all of the emotional experiences that are felt both mentally and physically. By paying close attention when the experiences of greed or anger are present, we begin to investigate what that state of mind feels like, where it arises from, where it goes, and how we relate to it. This takes a level of intentional *non*reactivity: we receive with awareness the state of mind and know it through direct experience, yet we allow it to arise and pass without trying to get rid of it or hold on to it. Rather than reacting with our usual attachment or aversion, taking everything personally and feeling the need to do something about it, we relax into the experience, seeing it clearly and letting it be as it is.

This is important on two levels. First, we become intimate with our mind states and with how they affect our mood and actions. Second, we begin to see more and more clearly that

states of mind and emotions, like everything else, are impermanent. With mindfulness we have the choice of responding
with compassion to the pain of craving, anger, fear, and confusion. Without mindfulness we are stuck in the reactive pattern
and identification that will inevitably create more suffering and
confusion.

This is certainly a radical practice, turning the mind on the
mind. It feels like a form of internal dissonance. In rebelling
against our mind's long-held habits, we are practicing cogni-
tive disobedience, the highest form of the inner revolution. No
longer slaves to the dictates of the mind, we gain the ability to
choose for ourselves how we respond to the thoughts, feelings, and sensations of being alive. When we break free from a
conditioned identification with the mind, we open a door to
relating *to* our minds rather than *from* them.

(See Mindfulness of the Mind instructions in the appendix.)

The fourth level of mindfulness is paying attention to the
truth of the present-time experience—that is, paying attention
to and knowing when suffering is present, when craving has
arisen, and when contentment and peace are being experienced. This level of mindfulness extends to all of the experiences we have, including the awareness of the arising and
passing of the hindrances, the senses, the noble truths, the factors of enlightenment, and the attachments and cravings that
keep us in ignorance of the truths of existence. (I will say more
about these experiences in a later section.)

(See Mindfulness of the Truth instructions in the appendix.)

All of the sitting meditation instructions are applicable to
any posture or movement of the body. Whether done walking,

standing, sitting, or lying down, mindfulness and contemplative inquiry can and should be practiced.

(See Mindfulness of Walking instructions in the appendix.)

Eventually all of these meditations become one. The mindfulness of breath and body leads to the awareness of the feeling tone, then expands to the awareness of the content and process of the mind, and finally expands to include all of the phenomena of the mind/body process. This is what the Buddha taught as the meditative training called the Path of Insight.

8. *Concentration,* or focused attention, is another necessary tool on the path to freedom. In the time of the Buddha, concentration meditation techniques were commonly taught. There are whole spiritual philosophies built on the pleasant experiences that occur when the mind is extremely concentrated. And it is true: when the mind is fully concentrated on one object—for example, on a mantra or a single experience— you will often have a very pleasant, blissed-out experience. This is due to the fact that when your mind is fully concentrated, you are no longer aware of the hindrances of sleepiness, restlessness, craving, doubt, and aversion.

However, when the concentration wears off, the mind is still subject to those same difficult experiences. Thus the so-called spiritual experience of concentration meditations is really just a temporary phenomenon of bliss or nothingness. The Buddha had the experience of the highest levels of concentration again and again, and he saw that it was ultimately unsatisfying and impermanent. A temporary state of concentration can't change your relationship to the mind. It can't set you free from the confusion and difficulty in life; it only allows you to avoid or ignore it temporarily.

Although the Buddha ultimately rejected concentration as the sole path to freedom, he realized that concentration was a useful tool, when integrated with mindfulness, to bring about insight and wisdom. Concentration is developed through giving preference to a single object, such as the breath, a phrase or mantra, or any of the previous foundations of mindfulness. As we continually bring our attention back to the chosen object, the mind becomes more focused and able to see more clearly the nature of the chosen experience.

Concentration is best used to see the impermanent, impersonal, and unsatisfactory nature of all phenomena. These three insights—impermanence, impersonality, and unsatisfactoriness—are the weapons of the liberating forces of the inner revolutionary. Those who understand the way it is, rather than the way we wish it were, are on the path to freedom.

After hearing these four noble truths and the eight factors of wisdom—the elements of the eightfold path—the Buddha's buddies all understood that he had indeed found the true path to freedom. They joined him in the spiritual revolution and set off to help spread the message of wisdom and compassion to all who were interested in listening.

This was the beginning of the unbroken lineage of spiritual revolutionaries, known as Buddhists, that continues to this day. The Buddha and his homeys then spent the rest of their lives spreading the good news and opening the door to freedom for generations to come.

HINDRANCES ALONG THE
REVOLUTIONARY'S PATH

On the path to freedom there will inevitably be many difficulties—places where we get stuck or feel hindered. This is to be expected.

The Buddha referred to five main experiences that tend to slow our progress on the spiritual path:

Laziness (sloth/torpor)

Restlessness (anxiety/impatience)

Aversion (resistance/anger)

Craving (lust/attachment)

Doubt (believing the mind's tendency to disbelieve)

Every meditator experiences these hindrances (and their many subvariations) at some point during the inner revolution. The most skillful way to work through them is to observe them directly and to recognize that they, like everything else, are impermanent and ultimately impersonal phenomena of the mind and body.

Laziness, along with such variations as sleepiness, procrastination, and avoidance, is often acutely present at the beginning stages of the meditative path. It is normal for people to find it difficult to stay awake during meditation. This can be due to actual tiredness, in which case sleep is the prescribed remedy, or it can be caused by a physical and mental resistance to the insights that are being sought. If you suspect the latter, then your practice must strive to arouse energy and to see through the mind's or body's attempts to avoid waking up.

Some of the simple ways to work with sleepiness during meditation are to keep an erect posture, to stand rather than sit, to do some walking meditation, or to wash the face with cold water. If you are plagued by sleepiness, it is important to understand that this is normal; it doesn't mean that there is something wrong with you or your practice. It is just a phase that will surely pass. Seeing it clearly as part of the path should help remove the judgment and offer the willingness to persevere.

Restlessness, with its siblings anxiousness, impatience, and intolerance, is also going to occur. Many people like to say that they can't meditate because it is too hard to sit still. But it is not the stillness that is the problem; it is energetic impatience and an intolerance for inner movement. During meditation it is common to experience the desire to be doing anything but sitting still. We want to be distracted and entertained; we find facing the mental and physical experiences of the body boring or difficult. As our attention runs after thoughts, ideas, concepts, plans, or memories, every cell in our body seems to be screaming for release from the torture of nonaction and nondistraction.

Once, when I was complaining about this very thing to my father, he said, "If you can't be bored, you can't be Buddhist." For those of us who have spent most of our lives addicted to intense experience, the more subtle states of existence can feel quite boring. Although I understand what my father was saying and I feel that it is a true statement, I also feel that if we are able to tolerate and investigate the moment-to-moment experience of restlessness, it is both fascinating and instructive. Rather than thinking that we have to get rid of restlessness, we turn our attention on the restlessness itself. That introspection often makes it clear that we are just trying to avoid some aspect of confusion, or perhaps the mind and body are simply craving pleasure and distraction from pain. Then we see for ourselves that restlessness is also impersonal; it is just the mind and body's habitual reaction to certain experiences. Anxiousness becomes interesting and fruitful; as we meditate on it, great insights begin to arise into the nature of the mind and body.

Aversion, perhaps with anger and disdain, is our next visitor. When we pay attention to our mind/body/emotional experience, we see clearly how much of life is unpleasant. The body is so often experiencing unpleasant sensations, the mind thinking unpleasant thoughts, and the heart experiencing the pains of the past, present, and future. Even just sitting still is uncomfortable for most people; and if the body isn't uncomfortable, chances are we're thinking about the resentments we're holding on to or some shame we feel. Each negative judgment of ourselves or others is a form of aversion.

Aversion isn't the enemy; it is just the normal reaction of the mind and body to pain. Whatever the hurt we feel— whether of mind, body, or emotion—our biological survival mechanism tries to get rid of it. The problem is that we don't actually have the ability to escape from all of the painful experiences in life. It can't be done. Thus the revolutionary's practice is to learn to break the habitual reactive tendency of aversion and to replace it with a compassionate response. The good news is that although aversion or anger toward pain is common but unhelpful, compassion is a response that decreases suffering and brings about an internal and external experience of safety and well-being.

A compassionate response can, at times, be as simple as seeing clearly the pain we are meeting with anger or aversion, and just letting go of the attempt to push it away and relaxing into the experience itself with mercy and care.

As with aversion, craving for and attachment to pleasure is a completely impersonal biological survival response of our human species. Of *course* we want pleasure; if we didn't, we wouldn't procreate, and that would be the end of our human animal existence. When we understand that craving for sense pleasures is just the mind/body's attempt at survival and happiness, it is much easier to accept and transform. The first step is seeing it for what it is: a natural phenomenon of the human condition. Meditation allows us to do this.

When we understand this—when we see that craving for and attachment to impermanent experiences allows us to survive, but also creates unnecessary suffering—we begin to let go or let be. In meditation we can observe the arising and passing of craving and see that it is just the mind trying to survive and find satisfaction. But the greatest satisfaction comes not from chasing pleasure and avoiding pain, but from the radical acceptance of life as it is, without fighting it and clinging to passing desires. When we achieve that sort of acceptance, craving is no longer a problem; it's just another thought, arising from nowhere and dissolving into nothing.

. . .

The experience of doubt, the final hindrance which the Buddha spoke of, can be the most difficult and debilitating. When doubts arise and we believe them, they have the power to stop our practice. Sometimes the doubt we experience is self-doubt—for example, the feeling that we can't meditate or can't change our relationship to the mind. Sometimes it takes the form of philosophical doubt—that is, disbelieving that it is possible to find freedom from suffering, or doubting that the Buddhist path actually leads to happiness.

Whatever the case may be, doubt is likewise just another thought, not to be believed or disbelieved but to be seen as it is, a passing thought. If doubt is a consistent experience for any struggling revolutionary, it should be investigated. Is doubt actually masking a sense of unworthiness perhaps? Or some old religious conditioning that says we can't experience true happiness because we were born into sin?

Buddhism doesn't ask for much blind faith. Instead, it encourages us to discover for ourselves whether the Buddha's teachings lead to freedom. But the path to freedom is a long one, and we must not give up just because it gets difficult or because our doubts become louder than our willingness to per-severe. Questioning and investigating are healthy processes; doubt, on the other hand, is more of a pessimistic experience. It is really the belief that we are right and the Buddha and the millions after him were wrong.

Perhaps these natural internal experiences of the mind and body are what became externalized in the traditional Bud-dhist teachings as Mara. And as I have already stated, I believe that Mara and the Buddha had an ongoing relationship—not just *before* but also *after* his awakening. This points to the hindrances discussed above as an ongoing aspect of the mind and body.

If you have been temporarily incarnated as human, you will surely experience laziness, restlessness, aversion, craving, and doubt. But the trained mind sees through the seemingly personal attacks of Mara, and eventually we can respond to Mara, as the Buddha did, with the simple statement, "I see you." Through the inner discipline of meditation, we too begin to understand that at times the mind will be dull or sleepy, or the body will crave comfort and pleasure, or doubt will arise. If we identify with these experiences as personal and as something that we have to get rid of, we will surely suffer at our inability to control the mind. When we see such experiences as impersonal and impermanent, we're on our way to knowing that while we can't control what arises, we certainly can transform how we relate to what has arisen.

Living a spiritual life that involves the practice of meditation allows us to come into harmony with reality. It allows us to see, just as the Buddha did, what is happening as it happens, with the understanding that the event or experience is impersonal and impermanent.

Or as Public Enemy #1 Flava Flav likes to say, "Don't believe the hype."

PART TWO

BOOT CAMP

Fundamentals of the Spiritual Revolution

So far, I have mostly been talking about the internal rebellion of the traditional Buddhist training in wisdom and compassion. But meditation is only the preparation for the external revolution. The point of our spiritual practice has to be more than just personal happiness. We must address the welfare of all living beings. The world as it is now gives very little support to such endeavors. Therefore, an external revolution is the next step on the path to freedom. We must now subvert and rebel against both the internal and external forces of greed, hatred, and delusion.

I must stress the fact that, although the internal training is insufficient on its own, we cannot skip it if we wish the external revolution to take root. We could look at the whole internal/external package as a rebellion from the inside out, but perhaps it would be more true to acknowledge that both internal and external transformation must take place simultaneously.

THE HEART OF THE REVOLUTION

The Buddha described the path that leads to freedom as the liberation of the heart, which is love. In Buddhism the words *heart* and *mind* tend to be interchangeable. It is said that some Buddhist masters will point to their chest when talking about the mind. The mind is not only the brain, as we Westerners tend to think of it; it is also the heart-mind, or that which in our consciousness experiences both thoughts and emotions.

The Buddha implied that this path of love goes against the stream. It is a revolutionary act to overcome the forces of greed, hatred, and delusion through the cultivation of their opposites: generosity, compassion, and understanding. Out of hundreds of meditation practices that the Buddha taught, he said that the most *direct* path to freeing the heart was the cultivation of loving-kindness, compassion, equanimity, and sympathetic joy. The experience of these emotions is our most effective means of dispelling the pervasive feeling that most of us have of isolation and separation. Loving-kindness and its kindred emotions allow us to enter into a divine abode, as it were; we experience a pleasant abiding of interconnection and nonseparateness.

Compassion and connectedness and their ilk are natural qualities within our own heart-mind. However, they have been buried beneath the survival mechanisms of attachment and aversion. The Buddha offers us meditative tools to uncover the heart's truest nature. These tools reveal a way of being in this world of suffering and oppression with a clear-eyed understanding of suffering, its causes, and the path that leads to the end of suffering.

Let's look at these practices in more detail—the Buddha's teachings about generosity, compassion, loving-kindness, appreciation, and equanimity.

Generosity

Taking the rebellion from the meditation cushion to all aspects of our lives is the task and intention of the true spiritual revolutionary. It is said that the first teaching that the Buddha gave to people he met on his travels through towns and villages was the importance of generosity. It's a good first teaching for all of us: in the beginning of spiritual practice it is our goal to break through our internal greed and self-centeredness by external acts of giving.

Generosity takes many different forms and can originate in many different motivations and intentions. Let's start with the practice of letting go of our self-centered greed and attachment by keeping in mind what other people need. Buddha said that if we knew the importance of generosity, we would never let a single meal go by without sharing it with someone who is in need. On this planet where tens of thousands of people starve to death daily, this is not a hypothetical suggestion.

Generosity is revolutionary. It was so 2,500 years ago in the time of the Buddha, and it may be even more so now. Most of the time people are so self-centered, so involved with themselves, that they don't stop to think how they can help others. To the masses, generosity is counterinstinctual. If you don't already understand this to be true, just look at the current situation in the world, and review human history. Our confused and misguided survival instinct is to care only for ourselves and our loved ones. But here in the industrialized West, we've taken survival to the extreme of indulgence.

To facilitate a change and to transform our relationship to that instinct, we need to constantly reflect on how we can help others. We need to ask ourselves, "How can I use my life's energy to benefit all living beings?" Meditation is one of the keys to unlocking the natural generosity of the heart. Underneath the greedy and selfish thoughts and feelings of the human condition lies a pure desire to help. We see this in our mindfulness practice: when we let go, there is a natural acceptance and feeling of care. But we cannot wait till there is no longer any attachment or fear to act. The act of giving is one of the ways to uncover the natural generosity that has been hidden by the fear and insecurity of greed. Each act of giving is a rebellion against selfishness. Each act of giving gets us closer to our true nature of generosity.

We can see the power of generosity in the Buddha's life. When the Buddha was enlightened, he didn't just hang around and cling to his freedom. Released from the suffering of attachment and aversion, he dedicated the rest of his life to serving the spiritual needs of the people.

While generosity is the natural response of the enlightened mind, as in the case of the Buddha, it is also the path to enlightenment itself. We are called to practice generosity even when we feel selfish. We are called to give even when we are more worried about ourselves than others. This points to the truth that our feeling of separateness is based in ignorance. Ultimately we are all deeply interconnected and dependent on one another. Generosity is not only good for others; it is good for *all,* including oneself.

It has been my experience that rebelling against the forces of attachment within my own heart and mind has been the most revolutionary thing I've ever done. And it's a battle that I continue to wage, one day—or rather one moment—at a time.

And though such rebellion is internal, it has external consequences. As Gandhi suggested, "Be the change you want to see in the world." If we want starvation and suffering to end, we must end greed and attachment within our own minds. If we do this inner revolutionary work ourselves, we can make a difference. In fact, it's the most important thing we can do for all beings. In simple ways it affects others. When we are less attached, we are more generous; and when we practice generosity, we send out positive reverberations (or at the very least send out fewer negative reverberations). Rather than adding to the suffering of the world, we manage to alleviate some of it.

Compassion

Another natural quality of the heart, compassion is very simply the experience of caring about pain and suffering—ours and others'. As was noted earlier, pain is a given in life. We all experience pain. For the untrained mind, suffering is a given as well. But with practice we gain the ability to choose how to respond to pain. Our instinctual tendency is to meet pain with aversion, try to push it away. Reflect for a moment: What is your first reaction to stubbing your toe? Most of us tend to react either with aversion (trying to push the pain away) or denial (trying to pretend it isn't there). The experience of freedom comes when, through the radical approach of the Buddha, we begin to have the appropriate response to pain, which is not aversion but compassion.

The word *compassion* can be literally translated as "quivering of the heart"—the physical experience of being moved by pain, feeling it and caring about it. Compassion pertains to both our own pain and that of others, both the personal and the impersonal.

For myself, this perspective has come from personal trial and error. For the first half of my life I tried to deny and run from pain. But pain always seemed to catch up with me. Eventually I had to accept that it is impossible to get rid of pain completely. Aversion, denial, anger, and suppression just don't work. Once I opened my mind to the possibility of compassion and explored the Buddha's practices, I saw for myself that when I relate to pain with friendliness and care, rather than fear and avoidance, pain is much more manageable and seems to pass more quickly.

Trying to push away physical or emotional pain is like creating a dam for the impermanent experience: it doesn't get rid of the pain; it just keeps it around for a longer period of time. Eventually the floodgates burst, however, and we are faced with the truth of our self-made suffering.

Compassion isn't some sort of highfalutin concept; it's a very practical and applicable relationship to life's difficulties. Compassion isn't our only option, of course, when we encounter pain, and for most it isn't our first instinct, but it's the only option that works to free us from suffering.

(See Compassion Meditation instructions in the appendix.)

Loving-kindness

Loving-kindness is the experience of having a friendly and loving relationship toward ourselves as well as others. The experience of loving-kindness toward ourselves is perhaps as simple as bringing a friendly attitude to our minds and bodies. Typically, we tend to judge ourselves and be quite critical and harsh in our self-assessments, identifying with the negative thoughts and feelings that arise in our minds. Being loving and kind isn't our normal habit, so training the heart-mind to be kind is another task of the inner rebellion, and another tool of the outer revolution. Mindfulness brings the mind's negative habits into awareness. Loving-kindness meditation is a way of creating new, more positive, habits.

As we see how much difficulty we create for ourselves and begin to respond with compassion, we come to understand that ultimately we want nothing more than to be free from the causes of suffering and confusion. As we gain insight into the impersonal nature of the thinking mind and feeling body, we come to understand that *all* beings would like this same freedom—an unfetteredness that we might call *happiness*.

Loving-kindness is the heart-mind's response of wishing that freedom and happiness for ourselves and all others. The process begins with a simple practice of setting intentions—that is, by wishing that we might be happy and free from harm. Rather than asking for happiness and peace from an external source of spiritual power, we uncover the heart's innate loving and kind tendencies. Through this practice of training the heart-mind to respond with love, and with the understanding that all beings are ultimately the same, we begin spreading love out and wishing happiness for all others.

Traditionally this is done by having categories of people toward whom we send loving-kindness in our meditations. We begin with our self, then move to sending love to the people who have been kind and beneficent to us. Then we expand to people we're neutral toward and friends and family about whom we have mixed feelings. Finally, we include the difficult people in our lives, and even our enemies, before expanding the field of loving intentions out to all beings everywhere—all of the countless beings we don't know or care about. The outcome of long-term loving-kindness meditation is the experience of friendliness toward all beings.

(See Loving-kindness Meditation instructions in the appendix.)

Appreciation

The next quality of the heart is appreciative or sympathetic joy. So much of our mental suffering is caused by the comparing and judging aspect of our minds—that part of us which feels jealousy. When someone else is happy or successful, we tend to feel angry or threatened due to our self-centeredness. Someone once said, "There is something not altogether displeasing about someone else's failure," and it is true. We often think, "Better him than me."

That is the opposite of the feeling that the Buddha is talking about when he encourages us to be appreciative of other people's success, to have the physical experience of taking pleasure in the happiness of others. Underneath our feelings of envy and jealousy lies a pure appreciation of the happiness in life. Cultivating that appreciation, bringing it out from its hiddenness, is a difficult but necessary aspect of the spiritual path of rebellion.

Appreciation balances compassion: we must acknowledge both the joys and sorrows in life. If we get too focused on the sorrows in the world, we will drown in the depths of suffering. The practice of appreciation allows us to acknowledge the goodness and pleasure that exist side by side with the sorrows. There is a Chinese Buddhist saying that affirms, "Life is made up of ten thousand joys and ten thousand sorrows." Compassion and appreciation are the only wise responses to those joys and sorrows.

(See Appreciative Joy Meditation instructions in the appendix.)

Equanimity

The Buddha also offered a teaching on the heart quality known as equanimity, a quality that balances generosity, compassion, and loving-kindness. When I first heard this teaching, I misunderstood it, thinking that equanimity meant loving everyone equally. But what the Buddha was talking about is a feeling of balance, a feeling of not being pushed off center by delusion, especially when we get into the realm of compassion, or caring about suffering. The tendency is to think, "I care about it, so I have to do something about it." People are suffering, so we gotta stop the suffering.

In his teaching on equanimity, the Buddha says the right understanding is that, although the appropriate response is caring, it has to be balanced with wisdom. Although we can care for and want to protect each other on a physical and perhaps emotional level, ultimately we can't do anything to take away the internal attachment and identification with craving and aversion that creates suffering in others. All beings have to do the work for themselves; everyone has to purify his or her own karma. We can't do it for anyone else, and no one else can do it for us.

This teaching must be understood on two levels. There is one level of physical suffering that we can and should do our best to alleviate. Then there is the more subtle level of internal suffering, due to clinging and aversion, that we have no control over in others. This second level is what equanimity points toward. Equanimity highlights the fact that only the individual has the ability to transform the relationship to the mind. We cannot force people to be free; everyone has to start the inner revolution him- or herself.

Practice in this realm of equanimity involves opening up to the understanding of the balance of compassion with humility. Although we may have the greatest intentions to free all beings from suffering—and there is a lot we can do through practicing generosity and kindness—equanimity shows us that ultimately all beings have to free themselves.

(See Equanimity Meditation instructions in the appendix.)

THE HEART-MIND'S LIBERATION

This path of uncovering the heart-mind's deepest generosity, compassion, loving-kindness, appreciation, and equanimity is the ultimate goal of the spiritual revolutionary. These practices offer us access to a safe home within ourselves. If cultivated, understood, and lived, they offer us a way to navigate our lives appropriately. They allow us to access the wise responses that bring about more happiness and less suffering.

I was first introduced to these teachings very early on in my meditation practice—first through my father's book *A Gradual Awakening* and soon after on my first meditation retreat with Jack Kornfield. In the beginning I thought that meditation was just mindfulness, and that all this compassion and love shit was something *extra*. I felt that the real spiritual path was only about present-time awareness and paying attention to the impermanent, impersonal, and unsatisfactory nature of all things. I was suspicious that perhaps all the flowery love stuff was something the hippies had added in.

As my practice developed over the years, I began to see through my own direct experience how these qualities of love and compassion were in fact a natural *by-product* of mindfulness. They began to spontaneously arise within me as I trained my mind to be present to the arising and passing of sensations. As I watched the passing show of anger and discontent, I was shocked to see that there were also moments of deep caring and spontaneous mercy. The heart-mind's hidden aspects began to be uncovered. And the more I paid attention, the more I began to see that underneath the fear-based mentality of judging and clinging, there was a purity of caring and kindness.

I have come to believe that these states of generosity, compassion, loving-kindness, appreciation, and equanimity are natural by-products of the meditative path. I've also come to see the real importance of cultivating these qualities, of putting energy into a systematic and intentional cultivation of these five heart-mind states. Why wait till they arise spontaneously if some intentional uncovering will allow access to freedom more quickly?

That intentional uncovering through meditation is facilitated by the process of cultivation and abandonment and by an appreciation of our interconnectedness with others.

Cultivation and Abandonment

By pursuing the heart-mind's deepest generosity, compassion, loving-kindness, appreciation, and equanimity through meditative practices, we learn to develop skillful mental states and abandon or let go of unskillful mental states. At first we may experience only how angry we are, for example, but gradually we may begin to realize that the anger is fueled by fear. Our loving-kindness practice will teach us to be friendly to our fears, and our compassion practice will allow us to respond with care to the suffering of fear and anger. Thus the unskillful mental states of fear and anger will be met with kindness and compassion. This process of cultivation and abandonment happens gradually, over time. We don't just begin to practice and immediately let go of all unskillful or unwholesome attitudes. The process takes gradual, systematic training.

The Buddha said in one teaching, "Abandon what is unskillful. One can abandon what is unskillful. If it were not possible, I would not ask you to do it. If abandoning that which is unskillful would cause harm, I would not ask you to do so, but as it brings benefit and happiness, therefore I say abandon it." He went on to say, "Cultivate the good. One can cultivate the good. If it were not possible, I would not ask you to do so. If this cultivation brought about harm, I would not ask you to do it. But as this cultivation of good brings benefit and happiness, I say cultivate it."

Though the process takes time and training, as noted above, abandoning unskillful mind states does not occur by force. Just as force is not the instigator, neither is fear. No, letting go happens when we begin to see, through present-time awareness, how painful the unskillful, unwholesome mind states of anger, fear, greed, judgment, jealousy, selfishness, and lust really are—when we see that the actions that come from these mind states are causing pain and/or suffering to ourselves and others.

The cultivation of wholesome mind states is likewise gradual. When we begin to care about others and ourselves in a deeper way, then the friendliness and love and generosity that are innate within each of us begin to arise. As we stop cultivating the unwholesome and unskillful mind states, as they gradually fade away, we begin cultivating the wholesome. Slowly, over years of practice, a transformation begins to happen.

Cultivating the good doesn't mean taking on virtue from outside ourselves; it means uncovering our own innate potential for love and connection—a potential that has been deeply buried and obscured through a lifetime of misinformation and not being taught the truth, through our own confused attempts to find happiness through sense pleasures, through hatred, through revenge, or through whatever our own particular top-ten confusions have been. Cultivating the good means recovering or uncovering the wisdom and compassion that are present as potential in *all* of us.

This means that we begin to align our intentions, actions, and mind states with a vision of the awakened heart—with what the Mahayana Buddhists refer to as our "Buddha nature," the innate potential for awakening. There is a natural awakened aspect of the heart that is within all of us, though obscured. The good news is that it can be unobscured. How? By walking the path. By putting into practice the values and theories that the Buddha taught and exemplified. By making the effort to abandon the unskillful and cultivate the good—and not just on the meditation mat but in all aspects of our lives. We begin with the intentional aspect of meditation, the formal sitting practice, but then we expand our intentionality to all aspects of our life, including the workplace and (perhaps the hardest and most important practice) our relationships.

Interdependent

The spiritual path of rebellion must include the appreciation of our interconnectedness with others. We begin this understanding of our interdependence through the practices of generosity, of not harming each other, of right speech and right action, and of purifying our minds through concentration and mindfulness. As we do all this we come to the experience of wisdom through recognizing the truth for ourselves. We become deeply aware of how much suffering is caused by the illusion of separation and begin to value the true happiness that is found in knowing how deeply connected we are with other beings.

When we know how deeply connected we are to other beings, we begin to care about their suffering. This is the experience of compassion. When we know how deeply connected to others we are, we naturally take pleasure in the happiness and success of others. This is sympathetic or appreciative joy. Furthermore, we come to understand the law of causality— that is, we see that all beings are experiencing what they're experiencing based on their own actions and not by what we wish for them—and therefore we relax in a deep understanding and acceptance of the way things are. This is the experience of equanimity. Finally, we take on an attitude of friendliness, kindness, and love toward ourselves, our friends, and even our enemies. This is loving-kindness.

The culmination of the realization of these practices was referred to by the Buddha as the "sure heart's release." The heart is sure to be released from attachment, grasping, and confusion. As I have already stated, these practices are both a means to this understanding and a natural expression of it. These experiences happen naturally and spontaneously, out of our mindfulness practice and the cultivation of present-time awareness; however, these separate practices can also be cultivated.

For many of us, depending on our own personal neurosis, there is probably one of these areas that we are lacking more than the other. This is the prescription given by the Buddha: to balance our hearts and train our minds to find true freedom and happiness.

LEARNING FORGIVENESS

A huge part of the revolutionary path of awakening is forgiveness. Henry Nouwen, a famous Christian mystic, wrote,

> Forgiveness is the name of love practiced among people who love poorly. The hard truth is that all of us love poorly. We need to forgive and be forgiven every day, every hour—unceasingly. That is the great work of love among the fellowship of the weak that is the human family.

Forgiveness is the journey and practice of intentionally cleaning up the stuff of the past that is sticky, that we have been holding on to, that has caused us emotional suffering. Traditionally this is done through the practice of repeating phrases of forgiveness toward oneself, toward those who have harmed us, and toward those whom we have harmed. In other words, training the mind to let go, to meet past pains with understanding and acceptance.

I feel that for most it is necessary to take forgiveness a step further. After doing that inner work of letting go, we must also take direct *relational* action. The process of releasing the heart-mind's grasp on past pains and betrayals almost always includes taking responsibility and offering forgiveness, and very often includes communication with those whom we have harmed, as well as those who have harmed us. This direct communication is the relational aspect of forgiveness.

Forgiveness is a process that continues throughout our life. We can't just say the phrases or do the meditation a couple times and be done with it. We can't just decide to forgive and magically let go of all the past pains and resentments. But it has to begin somewhere, and it begins with the understanding that all harm caused comes out of suffering and ignorance. There is no such thing as *wise* abuse or *enlightened* harm. This is the core truth of harm: it always comes from confusion. Anger, violence, and all forms of abuse and betrayal are always motivated by an ignorant or confused intention. When the mind is *un*confused, it cannot intentionally cause harm. The awakened mind acts with only wisdom and compassion.

That understanding of harm has crucial implications for us as we practice forgiveness, in that it forces us to distinguish between the confused, suffering actors and the actions themselves. This is perhaps the most essential perspective in forgiveness: the separation of actor from action. Whether the harm that requires forgiveness was an unskillful act that we carried out, hurting someone else, or an unskillful act on the part of another that we felt victimized by, we must see that the act and the actor are not the same thing. Most of the time the anger and resentment we hold is directed against the actor;

in our minds we don't separate the abuser from the abuse. But this is exactly what we must do. We must come to the understanding that confusion comes and goes. An action from a confused and suffering being in the past doesn't represent who that being is forever; it is only an expression of that being's suffering. And if we cling to resentment over past hurts, we simply increase our own suffering. By holding on to our anger and resentments, we make our own lives more difficult than need be.

This in no way means that we should subject ourselves or others to further abuse. Part of the forgiveness and healing process is to create healthy boundaries. We may forgive someone but choose never to interact with that person again. We must not confuse letting go of past injuries with feeling an obligation to let the injurers back into our life. The freedom of forgiveness often includes a firm boundary and loving distance from those who have harmed us. We may likewise need to keep a loving distance from those whom we have harmed, to keep them from further harm. To that extent, this practice of letting go of the past and making amends for our behavior is more internal work than relational. As my father likes to say, "We can let them back into our heart without ever letting them back into our house."

Forgiveness is not a selfish pursuit of personal happiness. It alleviates suffering in the world. As each one of us frees ourself from clinging to resentments that cause suffering, we relieve our friends, family, and community of the burden of our unhappiness. This is not a philosophical proposal; it is a verified and practical truth. Through our suffering and lack of forgiveness, we tend to do all kinds of unskillful things that hurt others. We close ourselves off from love out of fear of further pains or betrayals.

I have witnessed the power of forgiveness most fully in my work with prisoners. While working at San Quentin State Prison as a counselor and meditation teacher, over and over I witnessed deep healings of men who had committed violent crimes. As these inmates approached the inner pains of their past and acknowledged that their own suffering had been spilling out onto others, they were able to start a process of internal forgiveness and compassion that eventually led to personal commitments to nonviolence—commitments that in turn made the communities to which they returned safer places.

Some *actions* may not be forgivable, but all *actors* are. For the actor, the person whose own suffering has spilled onto other people, there is always the possibility of compassion. There is always potential for mercy toward the suffering and confused person that hurts another.

Early on in my own meditation practice, I clearly saw that I had been in a lot of pain for a long time and that my pain had affected others in incredibly unskillful ways. Then I began to see that the people toward whom I had been holding resentment had also been in pain and that they had spilled their pain onto me.

This allowed me to begin to separate the person from the action and truly see the confused being behind the hurt. This was the hardest part: not associating the people with their actions, but seeing them as confused human beings trying their best and failing miserably, just as I had. I found trying to take

that attitude toward everyone in my life incredibly challenging. It took years of trying and failing to come to a real sense
of this understanding.

That's a common experience, because forgiveness can't be
forced. Having held on to anger and resentment for so long,
we have allowed that reaction to become our habit. And
habits take time and intentional action to break. In forgiveness
we are retraining our mind and heart to respond in a new and
more useful way. By separating the actor from the action, we
are getting to the root of the suffering, both caused and experienced. This is a counterintuitive process. Our biological
instinct is to respond to all forms of pain with aversion, anger,
hatred, and resentment. This is the basic survival instinct of
the human animal. It works quite well to protect us from
external harm, yet it seems to create an even more harmful
inner experience. The process of forgiveness is the process of
freeing oneself from internal suffering.

At a recent meditation class, a student said that she felt her
forgiveness was a gift that some people hadn't earned. This is
a common feeling among many of us who have felt injured by
others. Yet does our lack of forgiveness really punish them, or
does it just make our hearts hard and our lives unpleasant? Is
forgiveness a gift to others or to oneself?

When it comes to forgiving *ourselves,* we are more obviously
both the giver and the recipient of the gift. We are stuck with
ourselves for a lifetime, so we might as well find the best way
of understanding and accepting the pains of the past. It is in
our best interest, and the most beneficial thing we can do for
others as well, to find a way to meet ourselves with compassion rather than resentment. Though this sounds simple and

straightforward, forgiving oneself is often the most difficult and most important work of a lifetime.

It helps if we investigate our mind's tendency to judge and criticize ourselves, paying special attention to any feelings of unworthiness or self-hatred. If we can bring a friendly awareness to our mind's fears and resentments, we may discover that our minds are actually just trying to protect us from further harm. The barrage of fears and insecurities may be a psychological defense system, an attempt to avoid future harm—a confused attempt, of course, because resentment and anger toward oneself never lead to happiness. But if we can understand and accept that we have been confused, we may find it easier to begin to meet ourselves with mercy and forgiveness, responding to the judging mind with the kind of gentle patience and understanding that we would show a sick and confused friend.

As I began the long process of forgiveness, I found it much easier to forgive myself as a confused child than to approach my adult pain. Recognizing that, I placed a picture of myself as a child on the altar where I meditate. Every day when practicing meditation, I sent forgiveness to that kid who became the man who had experienced and caused great harm. Gradually, I became friendly with the child in the photograph. I began to care about him and all the confusion he experienced. Eventually, I was able to forgive him—the younger version of me— for allowing his confusion to hurt me and so many others. From that place of understanding and mercy, I was then able to touch myself as an adult with the same forgiveness.

My experience with forgiveness is that it, like everything else, is impermanent. While some resentments seem to vanish forever, others come and go. The most important thing to remember is that we must live in the present, and if in the present moment we are still holding on to old wounds and betrayals, it is in this moment that forgiveness is called for.

There was a time when I thought I was totally done with forgiveness. I had done years of forgiveness meditation, had made amends for the harm I caused, and had come to a genuine sense of love and understanding for myself and others. Then, as my mind became quieter and my heart more open, more subtle levels of resentment began to show themselves. In deep meditation experiences I saw that I was still holding on to some old feelings of betrayal; the core parental issues were still there. So once again forgiveness was called for in that moment.

The experience of forgiveness may be temporary; more may be revealed. If and when that happens we have the tools to forgive again and again. Just as Henry Nouwen reminded us at the beginning of this discussion, *we need to forgive and be forgiven every day, every hour—unceasingly.*

(See Forgiveness Meditation instructions in the appendix.)

UNDERSTANDING DEATH

Death is certain, but the time of death is uncertain, said the Buddha. But who or what dies? Yes, the body dies, and the brain as we have known it no longer functions. Yet even the most novice meditator comes to understand that the essence of who we are isn't in these physical forms. And who we are continues. Death is only a transition from one form to the next. No one ever really dies. Bodies die, but we continue—and we

shall return to another form or realm of existence over and
over. The cycle of existence does not end at the death of this
body. We continue to exist until we have freed ourselves from
all traces of greed, hatred, and delusion. And even after freedom, when we have achieved Nirvana, it may not be lights
out. Perhaps all that is extinguished is existence of form and
suffering.

Death is not the enemy; it is the natural conclusion of birth.
It is perfectly safe—in fact, we have probably all done it countless times before.

It is said that we usually die the way we have lived. Fear of
death is just a reflection of our fear of life. When we have
clearly understood the truths of impermanence, dissatisfaction,
and impersonality, death is no longer something to be feared.
If we do not understand these things clearly through our own
direct experience of meditative wisdom, we will surely live
our lives in fear of the unknown. We will live in fear of death
and never fully be alive.

Accepting death allows us to accept life as temporary and
precious. Such acceptance of death allows us to finally fully
incarnate in this world of constant change. And until we take
birth, there is little ability to awaken and serve others. Our
denial of death is a denial of life. Until we acknowledge death
as certain, we will be tentative about all that we do, thus not
fully showing up for or participating in the work at hand.

In early spiritual practice people often have great insights
into impermanence and clearly see the ways in which they
have been asleep and confused. These initial insights are sometimes mistaken for freedom. In actuality, though, all that has
occurred is escape from a deluded state of ghostlike existence

into the realm of humanity. When we begin to awaken, we finally become human; we take birth and begin to face death. Although incarnating as human is a positive step on the path to freedom, it is only the beginning of a gradual liberation from suffering.

The Buddha included the investigation of death in his initial meditative instructions, as part of the first foundation of mindfulness. This is because before one can find liberation, one must face incarnation. The Buddha encouraged his students to spend time in cemeteries and cremation grounds, to witness and reflect on the fact that our bodies, like the bodies burned or buried there, will one day meet the same fate. As spiritual revolutionaries we must face death and embrace the preciousness of our time in these bodies.

(See Reflection on Death Meditation instructions in the appendix.)

PART THREE

THE FIELD GUIDE

Engaging Reality

I n the first two parts of the book, we looked at the philosophies and practices underlying the inner revolution and
then the outer revolution of Buddhism. Now we turn to the
practical issues of community, sex, money, and freedom from
addiction.

COMMUNITY

Both inner and outer spiritual rebellion are relational experiences. The revolution cannot take place in isolation. Finding a
community to practice with is important on several levels: we
need like-minded people to inspire us, to support us, and to
challenge us when we get stuck. The Buddha felt that community was so important that he included it in the traditional
ritual of "taking refuge," or committing to the path of freedom.
Committing to that path, dedicating our life to going against
the stream, consists of committing to *awakening* (Buddha),
finding out the *truth about reality* (dharma), and participating in
community (sangha).

From the perspective of inner rebellion and personal freedom, we need to form communities that include spiritual revolutionaries of both more and less wisdom and compassion
than ourselves. Those with more understanding become our
teachers in what the Buddha referred to as "spiritual friendships," showing us the path to freedom and inspiring us to do
the hard work of understanding the truth of reality and
responding with compassion to confusing and painful experiences. The more understanding those spiritual friends have,
the more compassion and kindness they show to us and
others.

In addition to helping us understand reality and respond with compassion, the wise beings who are our teachers urge us to continue the revolution when it gets difficult and we feel like giving up. This support for awakening in a world that conspires to keep us asleep is an invaluable aspect of any sincere spiritual aspiration. The community also serves as a teacher by challenging us in the places where we get stuck—that is, when we become attached or aversive—and it acts as a testing ground for any insights that occur.

Those members of the community with less wisdom than we have can be our teachers too, as can those who are difficult: we see clearly where we are on the path through our ability to respond with understanding and friendliness to those who need us or who push our buttons. Difficult personalities are a mirror for the places where we get stuck in judgment, fear, and confusion.

Since the freedom we seek is a relational freedom, freedom from suffering that is not dependent on isolation or silent meditation experiences, community allows us to put into practice wisdom and compassion toward all beings—even the annoying members of the revolution.

For an outer revolution to take place, the spiritual communities will need to unite. Positive change in society can never be facilitated by one person alone, or even by a small community; it will take the support of many, many people in a given society—at least a large community of vocal and engaged spiritual revolutionaries. The Buddha founded a spiritual revolution 2,500 years ago that was facilitated by the communities that practiced the path of kindness. The awakened hearts of the people spread the revolution to every corner of the earth, bringing about positive change in every society that encountered these revolutionary teachings and in some cases ushering in long periods of relative peace. In both India and Tibet, for example, the compassionate teachings of the Buddha facilitated a transformation from a warrior-based society to a society founded on the principles of nonviolence and generosity.

Positive change in society rarely takes place in one generation; the communities that we found and sustain are the legacy we leave for our children, and our children's children. One of the most inspiring things I've ever read was an interview with the Buddhist scholar and social activist professor Robert Thurman. Professor Thurman has been involved in Buddhism in the West for more than forty years. In the sixties, he was the first American to be ordained as a Tibetan Buddhist monk, and since then he has done an incredible amount of social activism. In addition to being a leading voice in the free-Tibet movement, Professor Thurman has taught Indo-Tibetan Buddhist studies at Columbia University in New York City for almost twenty years, inspiring thousands of young minds to awaken and to engage in positive change in the world. He has authored several books and is an international force of Buddhist awareness, largely influencing the popularization of His Holiness the Dalai Lama in the West. Among all of these personal, political, and spiritual accomplishments, what does he think is the most important? The interview I read recorded his response as "raising wise children." This struck me as incredibly wise, because it recognizes and respects the role of community in the Buddhist revolution. No matter how much positive change we create in our lifetime, what is most important is the legacy we leave behind. For the bigger picture, it is important to create sustainable spiritual communities that the next generation can relate to and thrive within.

Buddhist communities have brought about positive change in Asia for centuries, transforming violence and negativity into compassion and altruistic intentions. If positive change is possible in the face of the violent Hindu, Muslim, and native Asian religious traditions, it is also possible here in the West, even in the midst of our media-driven, capitalist, oppressive, Judeo-Christian culture.

The outer revolution will take place when the inner revolution has been won by several generations of antiestablishment spiritual rebels.

SEXXXUALITY

Of all of the energies that we experience, the Buddha spoke of sexual desire as being the strongest. Not just the act of sex, but the whole realm of sexuality, including intimacy, procreation, sexual pleasure, and loving relationships. The Buddha saw sexual energy as the strongest of all energies in existence, and perhaps the most difficult to relate to skillfully. This may be a little surprising, because when we look at the world we see a great deal of suffering, none of it linked in any obvious way to sexuality. Wars and oppression fueled by ignorance, greed, and hatred stand out as the most glaring defects of human history. A cursory glance at world history shows us mass oppression and destruction of life in wretched variety: German Nazism, the slave-trading of the colonists, the Japanese nationalism of World War II, the ongoing civil wars and "racial cleansing" in Africa and eastern Europe, the genocide of the native North

Americans by immigrants, the religious wars in Israel, the American invasion of Iraq, and the long legacy of sexist and racist oppression in all cultures.

Certainly this list suggests that hatred and violence are stronger than love or sexual desire. Nonetheless, I believe that if we look deeper, we will see that sexual energy is indeed the strongest energy in the human experience, and the most difficult to relate to skillfully. Although there is far too much tragic violence in this world, there are many people who are not touched by violence at all. Yet even if we removed all forms of violence from the world, people would still experience suffering in the realm of sexuality. Looking at our own lives, is there a reader among us who has not experienced some level of suffering in a sexual relationship?

The Buddha said that if there were *two* energies as powerful as lust for sex, no one would ever get enlightened, including himself. We can deal with the really powerful energy of sexuality and work with it skillfully, pay attention to it, understand it, and bring wisdom to it, but only because aversion, hatred, and delusion don't have quite the same power over us that the desire for procreation does. While the survival instinct our species has of wanting to procreate may not be conscious, it is certainly present in most of us on a cellular level.

Because it is such a strong desire, most religions and most people tend to fall on one side or the other regarding sexual energy. Either they feel it's all good and beautiful, or they feel it's really bad and ugly. Some say that sex is divine and the source of spiritual bliss, while others say that it's negative and evil, the work of the devil. I'm going to propose, and this is the

Buddhist perspective, that sexual energy is neither good nor bad. It is natural. It is neutral. It is just energy.

Assigning labels such as *good* or *bad, positive* or *negative,* means making a judgment. And yet sexuality is not inherently anything other than a natural biological human experience that is totally neutral. Well, perhaps it does fall into the pleasurable side of experiences, but only at a sensory level. Just because it feels good doesn't make it positive or negative.

Okay, so if sexuality isn't negative, then it isn't sexuality itself that causes problems. It's how we relate to sexual experiences that's important. It is completely natural for sexual desire to be present at times. It is also natural for it not to be present at other times. There are some beings who don't have much of a sex drive, but it is natural for most. In so many ways sexuality is just a part of our physical, emotional, and mental makeup. If you have a mind and a body, most likely you also have sexual desire.

The issue here is not sexual energy itself, then, since that's an innately human characteristic. The difficulty we face lies in our inner relationship of attachment to pleasure. On the cushion in meditation practice, we begin to understand that clinging, attachment, and aversion are the primary causes of the extra layer of suffering that we create for ourselves. We begin to see, through paying attention to the breath, body, emotions, and mind, that if we allow everything that arises to pass, we will experience a quality of satisfaction in pure awareness, in the natural arising and passing away of our mind states and sensations. If we let go for even just half a breath at a time, a relaxation happens, an acceptance of what is. If, on the other hand, we try to hold on to or push away certain mind states and sensations, we create a whole other level of discomfort and dissatisfaction.

Applying the practice of letting go to our sexual urges allows us to relate to the natural sexual desires that arise. When we are not being mindful and aware of the thoughts, feelings, and desires that arise, they run our lives and dictate our actions. With mindfulness and investigation, we can finally have the choice to act skillfully, which means at times letting go of or avoiding unskillful situations and at other times enjoying the experiences that present themselves.

If we look at our own individual sexual history, our own past or present relationships, as well as the relationships of just about everyone we know, we will see that these relationships have been the source of tremendous confusion and emotional pain. I think it is fair to say that a lack of skill in relating to sexual energy, whether our own lack (and resulting actions) or the lack (and resulting actions) of someone else, has caused most people to suffer.

As noted earlier, sexual suffering is caused not by the energy itself, but by our own inability to understand and skillfully deal with that energy. At its most unskillful extreme—as manifested in all of the rape and sexual abuse that occur daily in this world—sexuality is closer to violence or hatred than to love or beauty. But even those of us who are attempting the spiritual path—doing our best to pay attention, practicing our meditation and mindfulness, and trying to be as compassionate and skillful as possible—still struggle with intimate relationships, though such relationships are a tremendous source of joy.

Even in a dream relationship, one where you fall in love (and have your family, or don't) and live happily ever after, someone eventually dies first, and the other is left with great sorrow. Even "happily ever after" ends in losing your life partner. In *Embracing the Beloved,* a book on relationship as spiritual practice, my parents, Stephen and Ondrea Levine, write that if you really, *really* love your partner, you might want that person to die first so that he or she would not have to grieve your loss—in other words, in true love, you would be willing to do the grieving.

Attachment seems to be inherent in sexually intimate relationships, and therein lies the rub. The goal of unconditional/ nonattached interaction is simply unrealistic once sex enters the picture. Human beings naturally get attached to the pleasure of sexual intimacy—an intimacy that involves not just the physical pleasure of sex, but also feelings of security and safety. Even when one of the partners is unattached—or, more likely, emotionally unavailable—the other will most often cling to the idea that the unattached partner will change, and thus the clinger creates great suffering for him- or herself.

The problem of attachment isn't particular to sexuality, of course; it's come up in various contexts in earlier pages. Our lack of acceptance of impermanence gets us into all kinds of trouble. We don't like things to change, whatever the arena. But that attachment is a special problem with sexuality, because sexual desire and fulfillment are natural and beautiful and pleasurable. Of *course* we want the pleasure of sex and love and intimacy. But we don't want the experience to change or end, nor do we want our partner to change. We don't want to understand or accept that everyone and everything is going to change.

Sometimes people are fortunate enough in intimate relationships to change at about the same pace and in the same direction; they change together. They come together and grow, and it seems to work out. Other people allow some level of unconditionality around the relationship and allow their partner to grow and change without taking it personally. Most of us, though, succumb to the pervasive delusion that if something changes in us or in our partner, we are somehow to blame. We take impermanence and change personally, as if they were somehow our fault. Often our reaction is to hold on, to grasp at the way it used to be, or to fall into the delusion that we can change our lovers into the person we want them to be. We can get stuck in the way we want it to be rather than rest in the acceptance of the way it is.

The Buddha saw how challenging it is to be involved in relationships without getting caught—without getting hooked or attached and inevitably experiencing suffering. His response was to prescribe celibacy, meaning no intentional sexual experiences, including masturbation. Committed to the path to freedom that consists of nonattachment and compassion, he practiced celibacy and taught celibacy to the people who joined him in the monastic community. Because he realized that it is difficult (but not impossible) for people *not* to cling to the pleasure and comfort of sexual relationships, he said, in effect, *Sex is often a source of suffering. If you really don't want to suffer, it's probably best to avoid this experience. If you're having sex and falling in love and having families, how can you do that without getting attached? And if you get attached, you're going to suffer some. So let's just forget the whole business. It's too difficult. Just renounce it totally and let it go.*

Celibacy is a viable option for all of us. It doesn't ask that we do without love—that *would* be impossible—only that we do without sex. And love is something that, unlike sexuality, can be experienced without attachment. Though it may appear that love is inextricably linked to attachment, these two mind states are distinct. When we examine them with investigative present-time awareness, we see that there is a moment of pure love, which is generosity, and then typically there is a moment of clinging, often followed by demands for more; and the suffering of attachment follows. The reason it seems that these two distinct experiences are connected is that we rarely pay close attention and the process happens quickly.

While unconditional love can be nonattached, there is no such thing as unconditional *relationship*. When our love becomes sexual and thus relational, we impose certain conditions that are nonnegotiable. Fidelity, for example, and kindness and caring actions—if these conditions aren't present, the relationship will be a source of more pain than pleasure and will surely end in a broken heart, fractured spirit, and fatigued mind. Of course the conditions of relationship don't necessarily have to affect unconditional love, but most often when the container of loving sexual relationship is broken, the love itself is also somehow altered.

It seems likely, then, that no matter how good a meditator we become, in the realm of sexually intimate relationships we are going to experience some level of suffering. That is the "contract" we sign when we choose to enter into sexual relationships. It is much better to enter such relationships with an understanding of the consequences of getting attached than to be blindsided by the reality of impermanence when it reveals itself.

In my own experience, I suffered so much in my early life that I came to spiritual practice with the sincere motivation to find freedom from suffering. When I heard the Buddhist teachings on celibacy, I felt that they were too extreme, that too much was being asked. After all, I just wanted to find some peace of mind; I didn't want to become a saint or anything. After I had been practicing for a while, I found that the addictions, violence, and dishonesty of my youth were no longer such a source of suffering, though my life continued to be difficult. As my life slowly transformed, I became more sensitive about my actions and their effects on me and others. With that increased sensitivity, it became clear to me that I didn't have the ability to be nonattached in the realm of sexuality. In fact, the main source of suffering in my life had become my relationship to sexual desire and my unskillfulness in relationships. I began to see how often I was getting hurt and hurting other people in sexual relationships.

That's when I began to understand why the Buddha had put so much emphasis on celibacy. I also had a teacher who was practicing and teaching celibacy and I had been attending retreats with the Buddhist monk Ajahn Amaro. So out of my sincere desire for freedom, I decided to try the path of celibacy.

I was in my early twenties when I first took a vow of celibacy. (No masturbation, no sexual contact, no intercourse, no intentional ejaculation.) During the couple of years I spent in that practice, I found it incredibly difficult. I was very attached to sex and the intimacy, pleasure, and comfort that it afforded. Honestly, I probably put as much energy into not having sex as I had put into having sex!

But it was through celibacy that I first experienced transformative insights into the law of impermanence. When I learned to allow sexual desire to be present and to feel the cravings

without acting on them, I began to really understand the truth
of impermanence. No matter how strong the mind state and
the hindrances of doubt and fear, those emotions always
passed. At times it felt as if I was going to be alone for the rest
of my life, as if I would die of loneliness. Yet through letting all
of those thoughts and feelings come and then watching them
go, I learned more about impermanence than I had in years of
meditation. Eventually a calm and steady ease developed: I
knew to expect lust to come and go. I knew that I could handle
anything the mind and body presented, and thus I could direct
my time and energy toward practice and service.

Many people take the stance that because sexual desire is
completely natural, to suppress or renounce it is unnatural and
even unhealthy. For the most part I agree with that. If we are
suppressing or pushing anything away, there's generally something unhealthy going on; it's just more aversion. But celibacy
isn't aversion or suppression; it's the practice of allowing desire
to be present without acting on it.

When we practice mindfulness and allow sexual energy to
be the object of awareness, rather than allowing ourselves to be
a slave to the libido's every request, we begin to relate *to* sexuality rather than *from* it. When we aren't paying attention, our
sexual desires motivate our actions, whether we like it or not.
When we are paying attention, we can choose to take action
to fulfill our desires or to abstain. When sexuality is related to
skillfully, it becomes our teacher rather than our tormentor. It
becomes just another experience in the mind and body that
we can and should pay close attention to.

For Buddhist practitioners, sexuality is a dilemma. We have
a teacher, a model of celibacy, yet most of us aren't actually

practicing celibacy as the Buddha did. After I relinquished my vow of celibacy and entered back into relationships, I returned to the realm of relational difficulties. Some years later I went off and tried to ordain as a monk, thinking that I would go back into the celibate lifestyle, but I was unsuccessful. I knew that it was *possible,* but I didn't have the willingness. It felt clear to me that my path in this lifetime was going to be one of relationship and service and life as practice. So I left the monastery idea behind and returned to the world, convinced that that's where my work is to be done.

I feel very clear about the suffering that I willingly experience and cause through my participation in intimate relationships. It is very important for us to reflect for ourselves on the truth of this willingness and see that we are not victims. Those of us who don't opt for celibacy are choosing to participate in sexual relationships, knowing that difficulty is inherent in such relationships, and knowing that sooner or later we are going to suffer as the outcome of attachment in an impermanent realm. We have the option or model of not participating in sexual relationships. If we consciously choose a different path, choose to satisfy sexual desire and to participate in the most skillful way that we can in relationships, it is important that we know and acknowledge the price tag of this participation.

The Buddha's solution was celibacy, a path of both internal and external renunciation. Our solution may be the more internal path of renouncing attachment: we may choose to be as wise and careful as possible while accepting responsibility for all of our actions, understanding that every action has a reaction. But we need to make that choice with an eye toward karma—the truth of cause and effect. In other words, we must realize that we are consciously choosing to participate in a realm of experience that, however natural and beautiful and pleasurable, seems to inevitably cause suffering for us.

I can't say it enough: most of us don't have the ability to remain only loving and completely nonattached. There are Tibetan and Indian spiritual traditions, such as Tantra, that propose nonattached sexual experience as a path to enlightenment. My opinion is that those teachings are nice ideals, but they're not very practical. The Dalai Lama is rumored to have said that being able to have sex without any attachment would take the level of attainment of being able to eat either chocolate cake or dog shit without any preference between the two. That's an impressive amount of nonattachment! The Dalai Lama also said that he didn't know anyone alive who had attained this level of nonattachment.

For those of us who are what the Buddha referred to as laypeople—that is, nonmonastics who practice Buddhism and follow the Buddhist path without practicing celibacy or living by the strict code of ethics and renunciation of monks and nuns—all the Buddha really offered was the five precepts. He said don't kill things, don't steal things, don't use drugs, don't lie, and refrain from sexual misconduct.

What "sexual misconduct" is is fairly vague in Buddhist scriptures. It comes down to the general rule of not committing adultery and not intentionally causing harm through our sexual energy. The general language says, in effect, *Go for it, consenting adults—but be willing to accept the consequences. Enjoy all the pleasure and intimacy that sex brings, but be awake. Remember the truth of impermanence: that you are going to change and your partner is going to change and you are probably not going to like it. Be willing and go into it with your eyes open.*

I offer all of this in a spirit of exploration. I don't claim to have all the answers. I admit that this is the most challenging realm of my practice and the cause of the most suffering in my life. And I know I am not alone in that.

$$$

Money is energy: we exert our energy in some sort of livelihood, and in exchange we are offered currency. In and of itself, money is nothing more than paper and metal to which societies have assigned great meaning. Yet it has become a necessity for most of us. We need money to survive in the modern world. Regrettably, the human tendencies toward greed and jealousy often turn money into a source of suffering.

We are constantly fed messages about how money equals happiness. But money never equals true happiness. It affords us comfort and pleasure, but that is all—and pleasure isn't the same thing as happiness. The proof, should we need it, is that rich people suffer too.

As with everything else, money is not the problem; it is our relationship to money that causes us to suffer.

There is a common misunderstanding in spiritual circles that we should live simply and humbly or even be poor, but the Buddha made no such stipulation. He taught that we should either truly renounce all possessions and enter into full-time meditative practice or obtain our livelihood in a nonharming way. He encouraged his nonmonastic followers to work hard and honestly and to earn as much money as they potentially could, so that they could do good things with their earnings. If we are intentionally poor, out of some sort of pseudo-renunciation, we will not have the ability to practice generosity with those who are truly in need. Consider the following story, which illustrates the Buddha's attitude toward money:

A rich man once said to the Buddha, "I see that you are the Awakened One, and I would like to open my mind to you and ask your advice. My life is full of work, and having made a great deal of money, I am surrounded by cares. I employ many people who depend on me to be successful. However, I enjoy my work and like working hard. But having heard your followers talk of the happiness of the renunciate's life and seeing you as one who gave up a kingdom in order to become a homeless wanderer and find the truth, I wonder if I should do the same. I long to be a blessing to my people. Should I give up everything to find the truth?"

The Buddha replied: "The happiness of a truth-seeking life is attainable for anyone who follows the path of unselfishness (generosity). If you cling to your wealth, it is better to throw it away than to let it poison your heart. But if you don't cling to it but use it wisely, then you will be a blessing to people. It's not wealth and power that enslave people, but the clinging to wealth and power.

"My teaching does not require anyone to become homeless or resign the world unless they want to, but it does require everyone to free themselves from the illusion that they are a permanent self and to act with integrity while giving up craving for pleasure.

"And whatever people do, whether in the world or as a recluse, let them put their whole heart into it. Let them be committed and energetic, and if they have to struggle, let them do it without envy or hatred. Let them live not a life of self, but a life of truth, and in that way happiness will enter their hearts."

It is said, as was noted in the earlier discussion of generosity, that the first teaching the Buddha gave to people who came to see him was often on the importance of generosity. Even before he taught the four noble truths or meditation, he taught people the necessity of sharing with each other their life's energy. This can take the form of money, food, resources, or attitude (a smile, kind word, helpful action). He said that if people really understood the importance of generosity, we would not let a single meal go by without offering a portion of our food to another.

Heartfelt generosity works to balance some of the greed and selfishness that seem to be a natural part of the human mind. The practice of generosity offsets the negative karmic effect of all of the times when we are so self-centered that we forget others and focus solely on our own desires.

Money is a challenging issue in most people's lives. Very few people seem to feel like they have enough of it, even the extremely rich. I once heard that Bill Gates, when starting out in the computer business that he founded (Microsoft), had said that he would be happy when he made a million dollars. Well, that happened fairly early on in his career, but he didn't stop there. Did he reset his goal, shooting for satisfaction at ten million dollars, and then one hundred million, and then a billion?

When greed is our motivation, no matter how much we have, it's never enough. Some of the happiest people I've ever met have been the poorest. In my travels through Asia I met so many incredibly poor people who were still, despite their poverty, willing to share their time, energy, and resources with each other. When generosity is our motivation, we can find satisfaction in the simplest things.

FINDING FREEDOM/
BREAKING THE ADDICTION

One of the problems we face as spiritual revolutionaries is that we get comfortable. Even though we don't always like what we are experiencing, it is familiar. We don't like the dissatisfaction, the suffering, and the difficulty of life. We wish it were different, but we are so comfortable in it. It is all we have ever known. Like a child who is abused by his or her parents—a child who screams for the familiar "comfort" of those parents as they're being hauled off by the police for beating him to a pulp—most of the time we would rather stay with the familiar than face the unknown, even when what's familiar is our suffering. We are so used to our confusion that when the choice for freedom comes, we think, No way—it's too hard. Because the unknown is too scary, we go through our lives repeating patterns of thought and action even when they bring us pain.

We can also get lost in delusional philosophies that explain the difficulties of life. We like such philosophies because, being scared, we feel we have to have the right answer all the time. Many of the world's religious traditions are a direct reaction to the confusion and difficulty of life. It is difficult to rest in not knowing, so we create the delusion of knowledge. Humans devise creation myths, psychological theories, cultural norms, political beliefs, and religions, all in a vain attempt to appease or control their core feelings of insecurity and not knowing.

What Buddhism offers that differs from most other theories is a direct experience of what is true. Buddhism doesn't ask for blind faith or belief; it offers a practical path to walk. We cannot find freedom by thinking about it with an untrained mind. The untrained mind is not trustworthy; it is filled with greed, hatred, and delusion. Only the mind trained in mindfulness, friendliness, and investigation can directly experience the freedom from suffering that will satisfy the natural longing for security. This is the wisdom of insecurity.

In relationships we can often see the manifestation of this fear of the unknown. We go through our lives attached to our familiar suffering by getting into the same type of unsatisfactory relationship again and again. How many times do we have to fall in love with someone just like Mommy or Daddy before we acknowledge the pattern of seeking love as an attempt to heal an old wound? Does it ever really work? With mindful investigation, we can see for ourselves what our patterns and habitual reactions are—and from that place of true knowledge, we can then begin to choose our responses, actions, and partners more wisely.

Life doesn't have to be so unsatisfactory. This is the good news: there is a cause to our confusion and suffering—it is our relationship to craving—and that cause can be altered to bring about a different effect. Notice that I don't say it's craving itself that's the problem. That's just a natural phenomenon of the conditioned heart-mind. No, the problem lies in our *addiction* to satisfying the craving. We all experience craving. When we have a pleasant experience, we crave more of it—we wish for it to increase or at least to last. When we have an unpleasant experience, we crave for it to go away. We feel the need to escape from pain, to destroy it and to replace it with pleasure.

We are addicted to pleasure, in part because we confuse pleasure with happiness. We would all say that deep down, all we want is to be happy. Yet we don't have a realistic understanding of what happiness really is. Happiness is closer to the experience of acceptance and contentment than it is to pleasure. True happiness exists as the spacious and compassionate heart's willingness to feel whatever is present.

Though pleasure is in no way the enemy in our search for happiness, it comes and goes. When it's here we tend to grasp at it; when it's gone we want more. That addiction is the untrained heart-mind's natural reaction to anything pleasurable. This is clear in the Buddha's second noble truth: the cause of suffering is craving for pleasure.

Though we speak of, for example, drug addicts, what we are really addicted to isn't substances—drugs or sex or food or alcohol—but our own minds. We are addicted to that part of the mind that craves, that says we must satisfy this desire or that. Even in twelve-step recovery programs it is said that the drugs and alcohol are only a symptom of an internal imbalance. That's why I said earlier that our *relationship* to craving is the problem, not some substance itself.

And we pay the price for that relationship to craving. Our suffering in life is due to our addiction to our thoughts and desires. We wander through life constantly craving more of the pleasant stuff and less of the unpleasant. This is the place where spiritual practice as a form of rebellion comes in. My own experience, and the Buddha's "against the stream" principle, tells me that that it's counterinstinctual: it goes against our very human instincts to accept pain and not chase pleasure. It is a veritable internal battle, because breaking the addiction to our knee-jerk satisfaction of craving goes against our natural human tendencies. When life is uncomfortable, we naturally want it to change; when life is good, we want things to stay as they are. It goes against our nature to stop trying to satisfy our craving, to allow the craving to be there without reacting to it.

Few of us have the courage to accept pain as pain and pleasure as pleasure, and to find the place of peace and serenity that accepts both pain and pleasure as impermanent and ultimately impersonal. But our confusion may also go beyond the courage to train the mind. Other than Buddhism, few teachings even allow for the possibility of this kind of freedom.

Most of us have a fantasy of spiritual awakening as being purely pleasurable all the time. This fits right in with our craving for pleasure, but also with the creation of more suffering. The awakening of the Buddha within each one of us is the experience of nonsuffering. Not suffering could be considered blissful in comparison to suffering, but that does not mean that it is pleasurable all of the time. We have to let go of our fantasy of unending pleasure and the craving for a pain-free existence. That is not the kind of spiritual awakening that the Buddhist path of rebellion offers.

The important question then is How do we break this addiction? How do we loosen our identification with craving and the satisfying of our desires? How do we break our addiction to our minds? How do we get free?

The untrained mind, the natural state of human consciousness, has very little free will. We talk easily about free will,
about freedom of choice, but I propose that without training
the mind, we don't truly have the ability to choose. We are
actually slaves to, or addicted to, the dictates of the past, of
our conditioning—of our karma, or past actions. The Buddha
outlines this clearly and in great detail in the teachings of
dependent origination. This is Buddhist psychology. As we
saw in the earlier discussion of understanding, the Buddha
explains how we create suffering for ourselves, how we tend
to be victims of the past, and how we don't have free will
unless we bring awareness and attention to this process of
dependent origination. The short version of this principle is
that we have the ability to break our habitual addictive reactions through close attention to the mind and body.

The foundational practice is paying attention to our mind,
our body, and our present-time experience. It is hard to pay
attention, because we have to face some ugly truths and tolerate some discomfort. One ugly truth may be that our fear, lust,
or anger is all we see in the beginning. Since the mind does not
easily pay attention to the present, effort is necessary. The
mind, which is all over the place from one moment to the
next, has to be trained. The Buddha said the mind was like a
monkey swinging in a tree from one branch to the next. Yes,
that is what the mind does: it swings from one thought to the
next, from the future to the past, from planning to remembering, from self-hatred to grandiosity. To get some stability, we
need the intentional effort of repeatedly bringing the attention
back, of paying attention to the present-time experience of
breath and body, over and over.

In fact, we are paying attention to *something* all of the time, though it may be a fantasy in our mind, perhaps a daydream about a more pleasant future. Through redirecting our attention to the present moment, to the simple reality of our breath and body, and through investigating the feeling tone of each experience, we open ourselves to the possibility of freedom.

Right now there is the experience of sitting here reading this book. Is it pleasant or unpleasant? Are you meeting the discomfort in your body with aversion or compassion?

Bringing awareness to the feeling tone in this moment allows us to relax and release the aversion. Our habitual tendency, when there is discomfort, is to push it away, but the aversion to that discomfort seems to make it grow bigger, and pretty soon we begin squirming around or we feel that we have to run out of the room because sitting still is a pain in the ass.

Awareness of the desire for things to be other than the way they are is key. Thus the first step in breaking the addiction is acknowledging the unsatisfactory nature of both pleasure and pain. We do this by being vigilant toward and aware of the presence of dissatisfaction, the desire for things to be different. Yet we also need to pay attention to moments of ease and well-being, the experience of nonattachment, when the mind is free from suffering. We are usually hyper-vigilant when something is uncomfortable, yet when it is pleasurable or peaceful we often pay no attention, except perhaps to think about how we are going to get more of that pleasure.

Awareness of the lack of satisfaction and of the craving for things to be different allows us to take the next step toward freedom. We can relax the clinging of the mind and body and simply accept that we feel a craving for more or less of something. We can ask ourselves, "Can I accept this one moment at a time? Can I acknowledge that this is the way it is, and though I want things to be different, can I let go of that aversion and let things be the way they are?"

It is important to acknowledge this process as it is going on by investigating it and acknowledging our feelings of craving. Our conditioned tendency is to push or pull or grasp or run. The inner rebellion calls us to the practice of letting go or letting be. From the awareness of grasping or aversion comes the possibility of letting it go. With the trained mind, we can (at least at times) just release our mental or physical grip. Because all things that have arisen will pass, that act of letting go will allow the experience to pass. Letting be is similar to letting go: it means letting the experience (and all the feelings it engenders) be present the way that it is, accepting the experience as unsatisfactory, impermanent, and impersonal.

I often find that I am not so good at internally just letting it go or letting it be, but with time I have become able to tolerate unpleasantness without externalizing it and acting on it. For example, I don't have to say the angry words; I still experience the anger or fear, but I can pause and respond with compassion rather than react with angst.

The Buddha suggests that once we have acknowledged our clinging or aversion, if we can't easily let it go, we should try redirecting our attention to something else, to another place in the body that is not painful. For example, during meditation if there is pain in your left knee and you feel the aversion to it but can't accept or tolerate it, redirect your attention somewhere else; try, for example, bringing the attention back to the breath.

Another level of Buddhist practice that addresses craving is inquiry. We can investigate what is going on. What is underneath this desire for more or less? What is motivating or fueling this aversion? Why is this thought pattern being played over and over again? When I really start to investigate my aversion, anger, or lust, I almost always find that what is fueling it underneath is fear—a base-level fear that I'm not going to get what I want or I'm going to lose what I have. Sometimes it even manifests as a fear that I won't be able to tolerate the fear.

I'm not alone in this, I think. Underneath our ego and anger and lust is often the insecurity of fear, which we find when we investigate. Once we recognize it as fear, we can reflect on the fact that fear is not an excuse for inaction. We can then take the next breath or other action and learn to live with fear as a constant companion. If we lived our lives taking action only when fear was not at play, we would do very little. I certainly never would have started meditating in the first place or begun to teach. Almost every time I walk into the prison yard to teach a class, some fear arises, but it is not a problem, just an old and familiar companion. In fact, for spiritual revolutionaries, the wisdom of insecurity becomes our greatest teacher.

Another level of inquiry is to look closely at our mind to see who is experiencing this fear. Whose fear is this? Is it mine? Sometimes it becomes clear that the voices of fear are not even our own. We are hearing our parents, teachers, friends, or enemies. We have incorporated those voices into our psyche and have been believing them our whole life, thinking that the feelings and thoughts of fear were somehow personal.

On a deeper level, we investigate what this sense of self is that seems to be the owner of experience. Who is really experiencing all of this craving? It's really just the mind, isn't it? Just more impermanent thoughts arising and passing.

If neither letting go nor investigating works, another skillful way to address craving is to attempt to replace it by actively reflecting on love, courage, and kindness. Since negative mind states are still just mind states, we can try to replace them with positive mind states. The loving-kindness meditation practice (see example in the appendix) is designed for this.

Becoming aware of what we are addicted to and becoming committed to getting free from our misidentification with and addiction to our minds, thoughts, and feelings requires a level of renunciation. A level of being honest with ourselves and realizing that we keep doing the same thing over and over, and the outcome is unsatisfactory every time. Part of our work as spiritual revolutionaries is to break the denial of believing that things are going to be different this time. And then beginning to change our inner and outer actions.

Here is a simple story I've paraphrased from Portia Nelson's *There's a Hole in My Sidewalk* that points to the process by which these changes are often made. It takes place in five phases or chapters:

A woman is walking down the street and there is a hole in the street and she falls down into it and doesn't know what happened, and it takes her a long time to get out of that hole.

The next time she walks down the same street, she knows there is a hole there but she is attracted to it, and she gets curious and she falls in again, but it takes her less time to get out.

The next time she walks down the same street, she knows there is a hole there but she is pretty sure she can jump over it, and she tries to jump over but falls in again.

The next time she walks down the same street, she knows the danger but is still curious, so she walks up to the hole and looks in, thinking, "Damn, that's a deep hole," but she doesn't fall into it; this time she carefully walks around it.

Finally, she chooses to walk down a different street, deciding that she won't walk down the old street any-more because she knows there's a hole there!

On the path of the spiritual revolutionary, we need to have that level of renunciation—a commitment that we are not going to walk down the inner streets of greed, hatred, and delusion anymore. Of course it isn't so simple—our habits and grasping are so deep—but it all starts with the intention to change. To find new ways of relating to our mind.

All of this points toward breaking the addiction to pleasure and the aversion to pain. We each have to ask ourselves, What do we really want in our lives, short-term satisfaction of crav-ing or long-term peace of mind and the healing of the heart that will lead to wisdom and compassion?

When we choose the path of wanting long-term peace, free-dom, and true happiness in our lives rather than the short-term satisfaction of pleasure and desire, then the effort to train the mind is there. This has been my experience. When I really keep in the forefront that my intention in this life is to be free, then being of service and practicing meditation and doing what I do to get free becomes the only rational decision.

This takes discipline, effort, and a deep commitment. It takes a form of rebellion, both inwardly and outwardly, because we are not only subverting our own conditioning, we are also walking a path that is totally countercultural. The status quo in our world is to be attached to pleasure and to avoid all unpleasant experiences. Our path leads upstream, against the normal human confusions and sufferings.

At times "waking up" can feel isolating at some level. That's part of the burden of the real revolutionary. On the relative level we may feel separate from the masses, yet as the practice deepens, on the ultimate level we begin to understand the total interdependence and nonseparateness of all beings.

The commitment to waking up takes stamina. Steadfast- ness and perseverance are a necessity if we are to continue on a long-term spiritual path. I wish I could say that there's some magical secret to all of this, that *this* or *that* is what it takes to persevere, but I have no easy solution. What it feels like to me is grace, which is a very un-Buddhist term. Truth is, I don't know why some people get on the path and learn to see the ways we create suffering, yet don't follow through to liberation. It's a bit like some alcoholics or addicts who get sober and start doing the steps to recover but then can't stay clean.

Reflecting on my experience, I feel as if it's been some sort of grace that keeps the fire burning. The craving for freedom has become more intense in me than the craving for pleasure. I have been blessed with the willingness to postpone short-term satisfaction for long-term happiness. And with that has come a willingness to continue no matter how hard it becomes, to persevere no matter how scary or lonely it gets.

It seems that very few people that start this path continue it for more than a few years, just like very few addicts get sober and *stay* sober. There's the effort, practice, and commitment of following the path even when you don't want to do it; but that level is balanced by this other mysterious level, like some sort of grace. From a Buddhist perspective that other level is karma. Our own past actions have dictated that we are on the path and will continue on the path. In order to fully accept that, we have to understand reincarnation. Since I don't have any recollection of my past lives, I don't claim to completely understand reincarnation, so I like to think about it as grace. On the other hand, perhaps it is as simple as courage—the courage to begin, to continue, and to complete the task we took birth for.

I want to again acknowledge how scary it can be, on a core level, to think about getting free. Getting free from the reactive tendencies through breaking the addiction to the mind is like going off into the wilderness to a place you've never been before. Yet fear is, has been, and perhaps always shall be our constant companion in this revolution. It makes perfect sense that we want to stay attached to our suffering because it is so familiar. Yet may we be the courageous rebels who are willing to defy the mind's fears and attachments in service of finding a new home in the hinterlands.

Paradoxically, what we most fear is not darkness—we know the darkness all too well; what we are most afraid of is the light. The light of freedom shines from the unknown, undiscovered truths of compassion, kindness, appreciation,

forgiveness, and the wisdom to respond with care and understanding to all beings.

But like any arduous journey that feels like it will never end,
the Buddhist path has both rewards and a destination. Along
the way, as we face our fears and confusion, we begin to realize that the way is perfectly safe and well worth the effort to
persevere. It definitely gets less scary the closer we get. And
when we make it through the dense forests, we can enjoy the
views from a higher elevation on the path.

You may not experience much fear at the outset. Often in
early spiritual practice people get a pink-cloud feeling: the way
isn't scary at all, and life feels easier and more pleasant. But to
really get free, most of us will have to come up against terror,
deep shame, guilt, and fear.

If your spiritual practice is all pleasant all of the time, you
are probably not doing it right. And it may be that very few
people have the kind of commitment to go through a heart-
wrenching, dark-night-of-the-soul type of experience. Again,
that's probably why the Buddha described this path as leading
against the stream.

It is said that eventually we will understand impermanence
so directly that we will see death everywhere. The end of each
moment will become so clear that we will know the end of
each experience. It may be terrifying to see the truth of constant change and nonstability in that advanced stage of awakening.

The fact is, I don't know what it would be like to be enlightened because I'm not. I'm still attached to many things. What I
do know is that meditation and spiritual practice have lessened
the suffering in my life and changed my relationship to craving.

I also know that I am committed to continuing the path no matter how hard it gets or how pleasurable it becomes.

THE FRONT LINES

For a real revolution to take place, our spiritual life and practice have to be so much more than just getting our ass on the meditation cushion for a period of time each day. Our sitting meditation is only the formal training period in our spiritual life. Perhaps we dedicate an hour or two to formal meditation each day, but we are still left with another fourteen hours or so. As was covered in the earlier discussion of the eightfold path, our actions, words, and livelihood are all integral aspects of our spiritual practice. Meditation is a requirement and a necessity for spiritual revolutionaries, but we are not meditating merely to become good at meditation. And our intention is not simply to have pleasant spiritual experiences during meditation. We are, as Gandhi put it, attempting to "be the change we wish to see in the world."

The whole point of spiritual practice is to have a meaningful and fulfilling life of ease and well-being and to utilize our life's energy to bring about positive change in the world. The practices of generosity, renunciation, compassionate action, and kindness are the external forces of creating that positive change. As spiritual revolutionaries, our intention is not to live our whole life in silence on a meditation cushion; it is to bring the wisdom and compassion that develops in formal spiritual practice into our relationships with each other and into all aspects of our lives. The formal practice period teaches us many valuable things that then get integrated into our life.

That's why the formal practice of silent investigative present-time awareness is extremely necessary.

The desire to have insight into the impermanent, impersonal, and unsatisfactory nature of things is a noble one. But we must continue to, as the Buddha suggested, "strive forth with diligence." This is where the rubber hits the road. With the mind fine-tuned through meditative training, we then continue forward in the outer revolution of meeting ignorance with understanding and hatred with compassion. The understanding and compassion that develop through meditation's natural response result in wise action—action such as taking the practice to the streets, serving the needy, protecting the oppressed, and educating the masses in the universal truths of kindness, generosity, and forgiveness.

Through talking with each other and having community, we see that every one of us is experiencing the same things. At heart, everyone has resistance and attachment. As we saw earlier, this is the Buddha's first noble truth, that suffering is a truth of human existence. It happens for all of us and there is a cause behind it, which is the craving for things to be different than they are. So the pain in life is a given that we all have to deal with, but by our actions we add extra suffering and dissatisfaction on top of that pain. We see that it is true for everyone.

Stepping off the cushion, out of Buddhist boot camp, and into our lives, we take our enlightened understanding of pain and begin to react with more care, love, and compassion for ourselves and each other. Eventually this comes naturally. It is the heart's natural expression of our own process of liberation, our own inklings of freedom, our own incipient awakeness. With each moment of caring, compassion, and responding with love to ourselves, there is a natural unfolding or extension of that, which is to be more loving, kind, and compassionate toward others.

Once we have acknowledged how much suffering we've experienced in our lives, and once we have clearly seen how much suffering there is in the world, the only rational response is an engaged compassion toward all forms of suffering. As spiritual revolutionaries, we must commit our life's energy to creating positive change.

We must honor our altruistic intention to not only purify our own heart and mind but to actually bring freedom to this world by responding with care and compassion to the overwhelming ignorance and suffering we feel and see; by directly addressing, through nonviolent actions, the constant destruction of life; by responding with compassionate and generous acts of service to the fear and greed and hatred that pervade the human experience.

The compassionate response of spiritual revolutionaries is both natural and cultivated. It is a natural outcome of our deliberate internal transformation, an intentional choice to use our life's energy to not only free ourselves from confusion but to help others get free from confusion as well. To respond with friendliness and compassion not only to our own pain, but to that of the world.

Yet for many of us, the needs of the world feel too pressing to wait until a genuine compassionate understanding develops. Perhaps you have already been reacting with anger in an attempt to change the world. Anger is a very understandable and natural reaction to oppression. But anger, which is motivated by fear, is also a source of suffering. If we want to eradicate suffering, it makes sense to start with our own. But we don't have to wait till we are free from suffering to take positive action in the world. As our meditation practices develop and our perspective transforms, the old anger reaction becomes the new compassionate response. Outwardly, the difference may be minimal, but inwardly, there is a big difference between acting out of anger and acting out of compassion.

My feeling is that service-oriented actions must be an integral part of our gradual transformation. In the Buddhist mythology there are many stories of all of the lifetimes of compassionate acts of service the Buddha engaged in prior to his birth as Sid and his final awakening. In one life he was a generous king; in another a compassionate animal. Sometimes he incarnated in hell realms, sometimes in heaven realms, but his progression from lifetime to lifetime was always motivated by an altruistic intention.

Although different schools of Buddhism have different views on this path of compassionate action, I think all would agree that anyone who is committed to the intention of non-violent alleviation of suffering for all beings is what is referred to as a bodhisattva—that is, someone who is committed to waking up and helping others to wake up (in the Buddhist sense of being free from suffering). The path of the spiritual revolutionary is the path of the bodhisattva. On this path we have many tools: education, resources, protection from harm, and the ability in inspire spiritual awakening.

Knowing that we have the ability, on some level or another, to help each other alleviate suffering, we need through our practice to bring that intention into the forefront of all our endeavors in this lifetime. This is done by developing a sincere and altruistic motivation. To this end, bodhisattvas may say something like,

> May my life's energy be of benefit to all beings. May I be of service. I commit my life's energy to compassionate work.

The Buddha talks about altruistic motivation being a prerequisite to enlightenment in the eightfold path, when addressing our livelihood. Not only do we have to use our livelihood or life's energy in a way that is nonharming to really get free; we have to take it that extra step and do something positive, helping each other along the way. This does not mean that we have to stop our chosen career and become a social worker or dedicate ourselves to feeding the starving masses, although those are both good options. For many of us, that something extra may be just a shift in attitude and motivation, whatever we are doing, wherever we are in our lives. A shift toward the intention to respond to each person we meet with more caring, more kindness and understanding. A shift toward being more compassionate and wise with our life's energy.

Although our motivation to help others may be sincere, it is important to acknowledge that it may not always be 100 percent altruistic. There is often a mixed motivation for serving. Sometimes it feels as if we have to serve in order to forgive ourselves for the harm we have caused and the negativity we have created. Such a response could be motivated by guilt, but it could likewise come from a healthy sense of regret and a commitment to karmic purification. At other times we may be motivated to serve out of a desire to look good—to *appear* altruistic and thereby gain praise.

If we feel a drive to use all of our life's energy to serve, it is essential that we be clear about our motivation, even (and especially) when it is selfish. Serving feels good. We like the experience of getting out of our self-centered thoughts and feelings by focusing our attention on doing good for others. We gain love and respect from those we help. But we must constantly be reminded that, as the Buddha has been rumored to have said,

> We could search the whole world and never find another being more worthy of our love than ourself.

In other words, the truest altruism is to include oneself at all times, making sure that our intention is to serve *all* beings, not just others.

Once we have found some level of ease and well-being in life, due to our spiritual practice and service, we don't get to just relax and enjoy it. Knowing that the happiness and freedom we have found in life are very much a part of the fact that we've committed to serve all beings with our life's energy and not expend it in selfish pursuits, we continue on that path as a natural course of action, doing all we can to bring about positive change. After all, the point of the spiritual revolution is not about how much money we can make or how much pleasure we can experience, but about how we can serve the truth of interconnected existence and defy the lies of selfishness and separateness.

The transformation from a selfish spiritual desire (I need to do this for myself) to a more altruistic desire (I dedicate my life's energy to the benefit of all beings) is a gradual one for most. Yet when that motivation changes, it is natural to have a spontaneous prayer arise that says something like, "May all beings benefit from my life's energy."

This is the natural response of the awakened heart. The path to awakening our hearts is through caring, not only about us, but also about each other, about *all* beings. Our mindfulness meditation practice, our formal and informal training, develops insight into the three characteristics of impermanence, the nature of self, and the way that we create suffering. That wisdom is liberating, but it is only one wing of freedom. The other wing is compassion. For most, some level of wisdom must be developed before true compassion can be uncovered. Then their care, generosity, understanding, and skillful response to suffering are genuine. These are the two wings of the revolution: wisdom and compassion. Without caring and compassion, all the wisdom in the world is only so much more weight. It takes caring and understanding for a fully awakened heart to soar to freedom.

PART FOUR

THE REVOLUTIONARY MANIFESTO

Despite all the words this book contains, the essence of my message can be condensed into a fourfold manifesto: defy the lies, serve the truth, beware of teachers, and question everything.

DEFY THE LIES!

We have all been seduced by the world's enchanting offers of happiness through pleasure and accumulation, but they are lies, shams, fallacies. In order to find the true happiness and freedom that are available, we must understand this clearly. We must experience a revolution in our perception of the material world. Inside each one of us resides the truth; and however deeply buried or obscured that truth has become, we have the ability to uncover and experience it for ourselves— and happiness and freedom will follow.

The path to liberation is one of defiance and renunciation. We must overthrow the deluded dictators of our mind and see through the confusion of the world. This will take great effort and a steadfast engagement with our own moment-to-moment experience.

Every day we are lied to by the world. Our societies, our families, and our religions tend to be filled with delusional ideals. Human beings have created a deeply dysfunctional culture. The insecurity of the human condition has led to the creation of many violent religions and scientific rationalizations. We have been destroying each other and this planet for too long. Human ignorance is the status quo; even in the most highly educated or religious people we see the unnecessary suffering of ego identi-fication, lack of acceptance, and greed for power.

In America we like to talk about equality and human rights, but this country was founded on violence and oppression. Our forefathers stole this land from the native peoples, waging war on the rightful inhabitants of the continent. The history of slavery and racist oppression toward each newly arriving ethnicity on these shores has left us with a legacy of ignorance. Although some of the outright bigotry has lessened in our recent past, racism is still the substratum of our society's structure. This is not just an American phenomenon of course; in fact, our classist, sexist, and racist culture is quite similar to the ancient Indian society that the Buddha was born into. Ignorance is not just Western or Eastern; it is human. For the awakened revolution to take root, the pervasive racist structure of society has to be dismantled. This is what the Buddha began to do way back in the day, through nonviolent defiance and compassionate engagement with the system of oppression.

There is nothing incompatible between defying the lies of human ignorance and serving the truth of enlightened human potential. Defiance is renunciation: the effort of avoiding and speaking out against the causes of suffering is always going to be part of the path to spiritual awakening.

Religion, which was obviously created to give meaning and purpose to people, has become part of the oppression. This is true in both Eastern and Western religious traditions. The Buddha, Jesus, and Muhammad were all revolutionaries who critiqued and attempted to dismantle the corrupt societal traditions of their time. Yet their teachings, like most things in human society, have been distorted and co-opted by the confused and power-hungry patriarchal tradition. What were once the creation myths of ancient cultures have become doctrines of oppression. More blood has been spilled and more people oppressed in the name of religion than for any other reason in history! Although faith and religiosity are central to human history, it may be time to reject all forms of organized religion and to begin afresh with practical, applicable, and experiential philosophy. I would reject so-called Buddhism along with the rest, because much of what masquerades as Buddhism today is in direct opposition to what the Buddha actually did and taught.

The Buddha was insistent on questioning and defying the religious structure. He urged everyone he came into contact with to find the truth for themselves, not based on faith or tradition, but out of their own direct experience of wisdom and compassion. So the spiritual revolutionary must defy the religious structures as well as the material world.

We can look to religions and spiritual teachings for the tools of awakening—the truth does reside in most of the religions—but we must understand that all religions also contain confused traditions and lies that need to be destroyed by clear understanding and our own direct experience of awakening.

Defiance means standing up for what you know is right, rejecting patriarchal human dogma, and embracing the search for meaning with a steadfast engagement with reality. It means seeing clearly our mind's fears and attachments as impersonal, conditioned phenomena and destroying the misidentification with the mind's confusion. Beneath the confusion we will find the heart's natural wisdom and compassion.

The spiritual revolutionary defies both the internal and external forces of oppression.

SERVE THE TRUTH!

Service is at the heart of the revolution. A deep commitment to honesty and integrity is necessary for all who wish to make positive changes in the world. We don't have to be perfect or holy, but we do need to be honest with ourselves and one another. We must dedicate ourselves to finding the deepest compassion and highest wisdom, and from that place we can live in accordance with the truth of reality.

Our human society is founded on confusion, ignorance, and lies. The legacy of violence and greed that our ancestors have left in their wake is the foundation on which we find ourselves standing today. When we commit to the spiritual revolution, we commit to uncovering and developing the truth that has been obscured by the confusion of greed, hatred, and ignorance. Through meditation, wise actions, and service we will come to understand the importance of generosity, kindness, forgiveness, and compassion, and we will align our life with the truth of total personal responsibility.

Serving the truth comes down simply to living life from the place of positive intentions. This may be counterintuitive; in fact, it may be the most radical stance one can take. It means rigorous honesty to self and others. It means doing the right thing even when everything and everyone in society is telling you to ignore, suppress, or abandon the path of nonviolence, understanding, and care.

The truth is that violence is *never* the answer. There is no winner in violent conflict, only harm caused to both sides. *The spiritual revolutionary practices nonviolence.*

The truth is that selfishness and greed never lead to happiness or contentment. Greed feeds discontent. *The spiritual revolutionary practices generosity and service in the face of self-centeredness.*

The truth is that ignoring or denying the oppression and confusion in the world is part of the problem. If we're not part of the solution, we are the problem. *The spiritual revolutionary is engaged with the world and responds to oppression with open eyes and a willingness to protect others and alleviate oppression. At times this response comes in the form of education; at other times, in the form of hands-on nonviolent action.*

The truth is that we are all grieving the losses of the past. Due to impermanence, everything is constantly dying. There is sorrow for the loss of all things. *The spiritual revolutionary practices openness to the sorrow of existence, meeting change with understanding and pain with compassion.*

The truth is that pleasure is addictive. We are all addicted to it; we crave for life to be always pleasant and never painful. *The spiritual revolutionary practices nonattachment, breaking the addiction to the mind and enjoying the pleasure of life as it comes and goes.*

The truth is that our suffering is optional. In life, pain and pleasure are a given, but we create suffering for ourselves through our clinging to pleasure and aversion to pain. *The spiritual revolutionary practices radical acceptance, enjoying pleasure when it is present, accepting and caring about pain when it is present.*

The truth is that much of the difficulty and confusion in life is impersonal. The human mind and body are not naturally in harmony with impermanence; this disharmony is not personal, it is just the developed survival mechanism of our species. *The spiritual revolutionary trains oneself to understand the impersonal reactive tendencies of the mind/body.*

The truth is that freedom is possible in each moment and in this very life.

We have the ability to let go, to let be, and to respond with care and understanding to what is happening in each moment. *So serve the truth.*

BEWARE OF TEACHERS!

The Buddha's final words were an encouragement to his students to beware of teachers and to trust their own deepest experiences. In his final moments of life, when asked about who would replace him as the teacher of the way that leads against the stream, the Buddha said something like, "Be a guiding light to yourselves; continue forward with vigorous effort and steadfast commitment to the truth."

The path to freedom has been explained by the Buddha and offered as a practical experience. Obviously we need to learn the practices that will reveal the truth to us—but that is all. A teacher's role is only to point out the instructions and encourage students to do the work for themselves. A good teacher constantly empowers students to trust themselves, to train their minds, and to uncover their own heart's wisdom. A good teacher is nothing more than a wise and caring friend who has traveled the terrain on which the students are now treading. The teacher can point out the pitfalls and detours of the path, but we each must do the walking for ourselves. When we get lost, a good teacher can give us skillful directions to return, but it will always ultimately be up to the practitioners to be a light unto themselves.

The Buddha rejected the guru role: he was an educator, a friend, an activist, a role model, and a guide, but not a guru. *Guru* implies the ability to impart grace and to do the work for you. This is counter to the Buddha's insistence on personal responsibility. Shouldering that responsibility is part of the against-the-stream experience of awakening. We are all lazy and long for someone to do the work for us. We buy into the deeply held human delusion of externalizing spiritual power.

This must be understood clearly: *no one can do it for you!*

I urge us all to be cautious and suspicious of spiritual teachers. There have been countless betrayals and deep harm caused through the unskillful actions of teachers and the unwise or blind trust of students. A trustworthy teacher is hard to find. Train your own mind and heart and investigate and analyze for yourself all teachings you receive. Don't believe anything based on tradition or charismatic presentation. Don't even believe the Buddha, and certainly don't believe me. Study the texts, study your own mind, and the highest truth will be revealed. All of what you are looking for is here in your own direct experience.

Enlightenment will come if you work for it. The path is a gradual one that leads against the stream. One breath at a time we make progress toward freedom. From the foundation of present-time awareness to the deeper investigation of impermanence and impersonality, it will all culminate in friendliness, care, appreciation, and a balanced understanding of reality.

Be a guiding light to yourself!

QUESTION EVERYTHING!

Nothing must be accepted on blind faith. If any aspect of these teachings doesn't make sense when thoroughly investigated, reject it. If karma and reincarnation seem too mystical or obscure to you, keep an open mind and continue to trudge the path—but don't think you have to pretend that you believe something you don't have direct experience of. Eventually the truth will be revealed. We don't have to understand it all at once.

I like to think of the path to awakening as cumulative, a step-by-step progression, like going from A to Z. Don't think you must understand XYZ before you have learned the fundamental ABC's. As we practice mindfulness, the whole alphabet will begin to make sense. The teachings within the four noble truths and the eightfold path are the ABCs of the path. The training of the mind in present-time investigative awareness and friendliness will reveal the whole alphabet; all of the dharma will be uncovered in our own direct experience, if we are sincere and steadfast in our efforts to find the truth. Only when our fundamental wisdom has developed sufficiently will XYZ be clear.

Accept nothing as true, until you have experienced it as true for yourself!

OFFERING OF MERIT

It is thought that spiritual teachings such as these, and the positive changes that potentially take place within the individuals, societies, and cultures in which they are practiced, have a profound effect on the world. May this be true. And may any goodness that comes from these teachings be offered, in all directions, to all beings everywhere. May all beings be free from suffering. May all beings do what needs to be done to uncover the great natural peace of the enlightened potential within. May our life's energy be in the service of truth and the defiance of ignorance.

May any merit that is generated by these words and actions be shared with everyone everywhere, bringing about more understanding and less confusion in this world.

MEDITATIVE
TRAININGS

Ten to twenty minutes is a good amount of time to start with for your formal meditation, but eventually you will want to increase that to thirty to forty-five minutes at a time. You'll find six mindfulness meditations below, followed by meditations directed toward specific mind states.

MINDFULNESS MEDITATIONS

1. MINDFULNESS OF BREATHING

Find a comfortable place to sit. Adjust your posture so that your spine is erect without being rigid or stiff. Allow the rest of your body to be relaxed around the upright spine. Rest your hands in your lap or on your legs. Allow your eyes to gently close. Bring full attention to the physical sensations of sitting still. Allow your breathing to be natural. Bringing attention to your head, release any tension in the face, soften the eyes, and relax the jaw. Scanning the body slowly downward, relax the neck and shoulders. Feeling the rise and fall of the chest and abdomen with the breath, soften the belly with each exhalation. Bringing the attention all the way down through the body to the places of contact with the chair or cushion, allow your body to be supported by the seat you're on. Feel the pressure and density of the relaxed upright body sitting.

Bringing your full attention to the present-time experience, acknowledge the full range of phenomena that are happening in the moment. Thinking is happening; hearing is happening; seeing (even with the eyes closed), tasting, smelling, and physical and emotional sensations are all present. Allowing all the experiences to be as they are, redirect your attention to the sensations of the breath. Let the other sense experiences fall to the background as you bring the awareness of breathing to the foreground. Take a few moments to investigate where you feel the breath most easily (usually either at the base of the nostrils or in the rising and falling of the abdomen). Find the place where you feel the breath coming and going, and use that as the point of focus. (Choose one place and stick with it; don't jump back and forth between nose and belly. It is not necessary to follow the breath in and out.)

Breathing in, *know* that you are breathing in. Breathing out, *know* that you are breathing out. A simple way to stay focused is by quietly acknowledging in your mind, *in* on the inhalation and *out* on the exhalation (if you are paying attention at the nostrils), or rising and falling (if you are paying attention at the abdomen).

Of course, you will quickly realize that your attention will not stay with the breath; the attention will be drawn back into thinking over and over. In the beginning, the practice of meditation is often just the practice of training the attention to return to the breath. Each time the attention wanders back to the thinking aspect of the mind, gently redirect it back to the breath. (This natural process of training the mind is the essence of meditation.) It is important to understand that this will happen over and over. It doesn't mean that you are doing anything wrong or that you can't meditate. It just means that you, like all people, are so used to *thinking* about things rather than *feeling* them that the attention is naturally drawn into thinking again and again. Until you have trained the attention to connect and sustain contact with the sensory experience rather than the mental experience, your practice is just that, training the attention in what we call present-time awareness.

Bring the attention back to the simple experience of the breath over and over. Breathing in, know that the breath is coming into the body. Breathing out, know that the breath is leaving the body. Each time the attention wanders into thinking or to another sense experience, acknowledge that that has happened, noting the thinking or hearing or seeing, and then again return the attention to the awareness of the breath.

While you are training the mind in present-time awareness of the breath, with the mind's almost constant wandering and returning, it is important to bring a quality of kindness and understanding to the practice. Try to be friendly toward your experience. Of course the attention wanders. Try not to take it personally; it's not your fault. That's just what the untrained mind does. It will take some time and perseverance to train the attention to stay with the chosen object of awareness. It is necessary to be patient and kind to yourself in the process.

Easier said than done, I know. But when you get caught (judging yourself, being too critical, or doubting the process), attempt to bring a friendliness to your relationship to the thoughts. And then simply redirect the attention back to the breath.

2. MINDFULNESS OF THE BREATH AND BODY

Begin the same way you did in the first meditation, finding a comfortable place to sit, closing the eyes, and relaxing the body.

Bringing attention to the sensations of breath, continue redirecting the attention to the breath each time it wanders. Continue to be as friendly and kind as possible to your mind's tendency to wander.

After about ten minutes of focusing the attention on the breath, begin to expand the attention to the whole body. Bring attention to your posture. Feel the pressure of your body on the cushion or chair. Feel the contact points of your hands touching your legs or resting in your lap. Direct the attention to sensations in the body of sitting.

With the foundation of present-time awareness, as established by the continual returning of the attention to the breath and body, you can now allow the attention to expand to include all of the sense doors.

Begin with the awareness of hearing. When you become aware of a sound, simply pay attention to the experience of hearing—the bare experience of sound being received by the eardrum. Although the mind wants to instantly name the object being heard, the direct experience is just variations of sound. Using memory and conditioning, the mind immediately tries to label the sound as a car passing by, or the wind in the trees, or the refrigerator turning on. In this level of practice, try to see the difference between the direct experience of sound and the mind's conditioned labeling of the experience. Keep it simple; it is just hearing.

Expand your attention to seeing, tasting, and smelling in the same way. Just seeing and the direct experience of what's being seen—color, shape, form, etc. Just taste. Just smelling.

Notice how quickly the mind names and classifies things based on memory. This level of mindfulness allows us to see how the mind is constantly trying to sort and name experiences based on memory, rarely allowing for new or fresh perspectives.

When the attention gets drawn back into thinking, simply return it to the breath. Then continue to extend mindfulness to the direct, moment-to-moment sensory experience of the whole body.

Allow the attention to be drawn to whatever experience in the body is predominant. When sounds arise, know them as hearing. When visions arise, know them as seeing. Don't settle for the mind's labels and conventions. Experience each moment as if it were the first sensation of its kind ever. Bring childlike interest and curiosity to your present-time experience. What does this moment feel like? What is the temperature, texture, or pressure of this sensory experience?

Continue to connect the attention with the felt sense of the breath and body. Begin refining the attention to the moment-to-moment flux of sensations. Investigate the constantly changing nature of each experience.

With clear comprehension receive the transient phenomena with nonjudgmental awareness. Attempt to sustain awareness of the arising and passing of each chosen sensation.

Continue redirecting the attention and reconnecting with the present moment each time the attention is drawn back into the contents of the thinking mind.

Attempt to rest in the direct experience of the breath and body, relaxing into the present-time awareness of impermanence.

3. MINDFULNESS OF THE FEELING TONE

After establishing some ability to sustain attention, you can begin to investigate the "feeling tone" of each experience. Whether you are paying attention to the breath or sensations in the body, each experience has a feeling tone of pleasantness, unpleasantness, or neutrality. By focusing the attention a little bit more and opening your awareness to the subtle levels of pleasant and unpleasant tones of experience, you bring mind-fulness to your craving for pleasure and aversion to pain. Feel-ing tone is the place where one gets attached or aversive.

Begin by practicing the first two meditations. Always begin sitting meditation by focusing on the present-time experience of the body. This allows the attention to settle in the here and now. As a basic guideline, ten to twenty minutes of breath/body awareness is a good idea before expanding to this next level of practice. (The amount of time depends on one's ability to concentrate.)

While sitting with awareness focused on the body, refine the attention to the feeling tone of your experience. Investigate and inquire into the nature of the experience you are paying attention to. Is this a pleasant feeling? Does it feel good? Or is it an uncomfortable experience. Are you resisting the present feeling? Bring mindfulness to the feeling itself; see for yourself how you relate to pleasure and pain.

What does your mind do when the present-time experience is neutral? Are you able to hang out with experiences that have no pleasure or pain associated with them? Or does the mind get bored and seek a pleasurable or painful memory or plan?

Continue training the mind in this way. Each time the atten-tion wanders, gently return to the present moment and con-tinue investigating your inner relationship to the pleasant, unpleasant, or neutral tone of each moment.

When you become aware of attachment to a pleasurable experience, attempt to let go. Release the mind/body's grip by softening and relaxing into each moment. Allow yourself to fully experience and enjoy the pleasure as it comes and goes.

When you become aware of aversion to an unpleasant experience, attempt to meet it with mercy and friendliness. Allow the pain or discomfort to be present, and meet it with the understanding that it will pass if you just allow it to come through the mind/body without trying to resist it, suppress it, or control it.

When you are meditating on neutral phenomena, attempt to relax into the absence of suffering. Tolerate the mind's craving for pleasure and continue to enjoy the experience of just being. Learning to enjoy the absence of pleasure and pain is key on the meditative path.

4. MINDFULNESS OF THE MIND

Part 1: Process

From the foundation of present-time investigative awareness that is infused with the intention of kindness and understanding, you can turn your attention on the mind itself.

After having established awareness of the breath/body and the feeling tone of the present moment, expand the attention to the process of the thinking mind. Observe the arising and passing of thoughts. Allow the awareness to be expansive: try not to get caught in the content of the thoughts; let go of the need to solve any problems or make any plans. Just relax into the present-time awareness of thoughts coming and going.

Break the addiction to the contents of and identification with your mind. Meditate on the mind as a process. Each thought is like a bubble floating through the spaciousness of awareness. One may contain a plan, another a memory, and yet another a judgment or emotion. Allow each thought to pass without getting into the bubble or floating off with it.

Until the meditation practice has matured, you will get seduced by the thinking mind over and over, floating off into a plan or memory that feels too important to let pass. Or all of a sudden you will have what seems like the most important revelation or inspiration. This is the natural process of training the mind and transforming your relationship to the contents of your mind. As with the breath, simply let go and return to the present over and over, bursting the bubble and redirecting the attention to the process again and again.

If there is a foundation of attention that is concentrated and stable, you may be able to experience the completely impersonal phenomenon of the proliferation of thoughts. You may see that one thought that arises leads to the next and the next and the next, until all of a sudden the mind is off in some fantasy, each bubble giving birth to the next.

Part 2: Content

After establishing awareness of the breath/body and feeling tone of the present moment, after expanding the attention to the process of the thinking mind and observing the arising and passing of thoughts, bring attention to the contents of each mind-moment. Know directly the truth of each thought. Be aware of each memory as a memory, and when a plan arises in the mind, know it as a plan—perhaps noting "past" and "future."

Be aware of the arising of all emotion. If fear, anger, sadness, love, caring, envy, empathy, or any other feeling arises, experience it directly; know that it originated in the mind and has manifested in the body as well. You may see that fear is an underlying motivator for much of the contents of the mind. See for yourself what is true about your mind.

Know each experience as it is. Observe the tendency to avoid, suppress, ignore, or resist the unpleasant thoughts, and recognize that as aversion. Observe the tendency to cling, crave, and feed the thoughts that are pleasant or that you feel will lead to more safety or happiness, and know that experience as attachment.

5. MINDFULNESS OF THE TRUTH

The fifth level of mindfulness meditation is bringing awareness to the truth of the present moment. Through the introspective practice of present-time awareness we can bring attention to the truth of suffering, its causes, and the experience of freedom from suffering and confusion. At this level, we can pay attention to and know when suffering is present, when craving has arisen, and when contentment and peace are being experienced. This level of mindfulness extends to all of the experiences we have. Traditionally this includes the awareness of the arising and passing of the hindrances, the senses, the noble truths, the factors of enlightenment, and the attachments and cravings that keep us in ignorance of the truths of existence.

While sitting in meditation, expand the attention to the whole mind and body. Know your experience as it is. When you become aware of the hindrances of sleepiness, restlessness, craving, aversion, or doubt, simply pay direct attention to the truth of these experiences. What does it feel like in the body? Where do you physically experience restlessness, sleepiness, aversion, or craving? Is the experience constant or constantly changing?

Likewise with the factors of awakening: when mindfulness, concentration, investigation, energy, joy, equanimity, and relaxation arise, take them as the object of meditation. Investigate and contemplate the truth of each moment as it manifests in the body and mind.

On this level of meditative practice it is important to keep the intention of objective friendliness. Meet each experience with acceptance and curiosity: "So this is suffering; hello attachment; hello craving. You feel like a tightness in my jaw, a hardness in my belly, and an abusive voice in my mind."

6. MINDFULNESS OF WALKING

When walking, know that you are walking—that's the goal of this meditation.

Find a place to walk that is twenty or thirty feet long. Standing at the beginning of the path, bring full attention to the body. Feel the feet firmly planted on the ground. Allow the breath to be natural, and contemplate walking. As you intentionally begin to walk, bring attention to your feet; feel the pressure and movement of each step. Notice the balancing act that the body does as each step shifts the body's weight from side to side. Your hands can fall wherever is easy and natural. Your eyes don't need to be looking at your feet or closed in order to pay attention to the experience of mindful walking; it is usually best to keep them focused a few feet in front of you on the walking terrain.

When the attention is drawn back into thinking about something else, pause and acknowledge that you have lost mindfulness of walking. Note where the attention was drawn and then continue down the path, placing about 80 percent of your attention in the body (especially the feet) and 20 percent on your surroundings. Acknowledge seeing, and note how the mind tends to instantly label all forms: grass, carpet, floor, dirt, and so on.

When you reach the end of the path you have chosen, again pause and feel both feet on the ground. Bringing full attention to the experience of standing, this is now standing meditation. Then intentionally turn around, bringing attention to the balancing act of turning the body, the swiveling of the feet, and the redistribution of weight.

Facing the path you just walked down, begin walking toward the other end. Repeat the process of walking back and forth along this path as a meditative training in present-time awareness. Find a pace that fits your energy and intention of moment-to-moment awareness. Walking slowly may facilitate a more precise experience of the constantly changing physical phenomena of the body. Walking at a normal pace or quickly may be useful for integrating mindfulness into daily life and the fast-paced, busy lives most of us lead.

COMPASSION MEDITATION

Find a comfortable place to sit, and allow your attention to settle into the present-time experience of the body. Relax any physical tension that is being held in the body by softening the belly; relax the eyes and jaw and allow your shoulders to naturally fall away from the head.

After a short period of settling into present-time awareness, begin to reflect on your deepest desire for happiness and freedom from suffering. Allow your heart's truest longing for truth and well-being to come into consciousness. With each breath, breathe into the heart's center the acknowledgment of your wish to be free from harm, to be safe, protected, and to experience compassion for all beings.

Slowly begin to offer yourself compassionate phrases with the intention to uncover the heart's sometimes-hidden caring and friendly response. Your phrases can be as simple as the following:

"May I learn to care about suffering and confusion."
"May I respond with mercy and empathy to pain."
"May I be filled with compassion."

If those phrases do not mean anything to you, create your own words to meditate on. Find a few simple phrases that have a compassionate and merciful intention, and slowly begin to offer these well wishes to your self.

As you sit in meditation repeating these phrases in your mind, the attention will be drawn back, as in mindfulness meditation, into thinking about other things or resisting and judging the practice or your capacity for compassion. It takes a gentle and persistent effort to return to the next phrase each time the attention wanders:

"May I learn to care about suffering and confusion." Feel the breath and the body's response to each phrase.
"May I respond with mercy and empathy to pain." Notice where the mind goes with each phrase.
"May I be filled with compassion." Allow the mind and body to relax into the reverberations of each phrase.

Simply repeat these phrases over and over to yourself like a kind of mantra or statement of positive intention. But don't expect to instantly feel compassionate through this practice. Sometimes all we see is our lack of compassion and the judging mind's resistance. Simply acknowledge what is happening and continue to repeat the phrases, being as friendly and merciful with yourself as possible in the process.

After a few minutes of sending these compassionate phrases to yourself, bring attention back to your breath and body, again relaxing into the posture.

Then bring someone to mind who has been beneficial for you to know or know of, someone who has inspired you or shown you great compassion. Recognizing that just as you wish to be cared for and understood that benefactor too shares the universal desire to be met with compassion, begin offering him or her the caring phrases. Slowly repeat each phrase with that person in mind as the object of your well-wishing:

"Just as I wish to learn to care about suffering and confusion, to respond with mercy and empathy to pain, and
to be filled with compassion, may you learn to care
about suffering and confusion."
"May you respond with mercy and empathy to pain."
"May you be filled with compassion."

Continue offering these phrases from your heart to your
benefactor's, developing the feeling of compassion in relationship to the pain of others. When the mind gets lost in a story,
memory, or fantasy, simply return to the practice. Begin again
offering mercy and care to the benefactor.

After a few minutes of sending compassion to the benefactor, let him or her go and return to your direct experience of
the breath and body. Pay extra attention to your heart or emotional experience.

Then bring to mind someone whom you do not know well,
someone who is neutral. Someone you neither love nor hate—
perhaps someone you don't know at all, a person you saw
during your day, walking down the street or in line at the
market. With the understanding that the desire for freedom
from suffering is universal, begin offering that neutral person
the compassionate phrases:

"May you learn to care about suffering and confusion."
"May you respond with mercy and empathy to pain."
"May you be filled with compassion."

After a few minutes of sending compassion to the neutral
person, bring attention back to your breath and body. Then

expand the practice to include family and friends toward whom your feelings may be mixed, both loving and judgmental:

"May you all learn to care about suffering and confusion."
"May you all respond with mercy and empathy to pain."
"May you all be filled with compassion."

After a few minutes of sending compassion to the mixed category, bring attention back to your breath and body. Then expand the practice to include the difficult people in your life and in the world. (By *difficult* I mean those whom you have put out of your heart, those toward whom you hold resentment.)

With even the most basic understanding of human nature, it will become clear that all beings wish to be met with compassion; all beings—even the annoying, unskillful, violent, confused, and unkind—wish to be free from suffering. With this in mind, and with the intention to free yourself from hatred, fear, and ill will, allow someone who is a source of difficulty in your mind or heart to be the object of your compassion meditation, meeting that person with the same phrases and paying close attention to your heart-mind's response:

"May you learn to care about suffering and confusion."
"May you respond with mercy and empathy to pain."
"May you be filled with compassion."

After a few minutes of practice in the direction of difficult people, begin to expand the field of compassion to all those who are in your immediate vicinity. Start by sending compassionate phrases to anyone in your home or building at the time of practice. Then gradually expand to those in your town or city, allowing your positive intention for meeting everyone with compassion to spread out in all directions.

Imagine covering the whole world with these positive thoughts. Send compassion to the north and south, east and west. Radiate an open heart and fearless mind to all beings in existence—those above and below, the seen and the unseen, those being born and those who are dying. With a boundless and friendly intention, begin to repeat the phrases:

"May all beings learn to care about suffering and confu-
   sion."
"May all beings respond with mercy and empathy to pain."
"May all beings be filled with compassion."

After a few minutes of sending compassion to all beings everywhere, simply let go of the phrases and bring attention back to your breath and body, investigating the sensations and emotions that are present now. Then, whenever you are ready, allow your eyes to open and your attention to come back to your surroundings.

LOVING-KINDNESS MEDITATION

Find a comfortable place to sit, and allow your attention to settle into the present-time experience of the body. Relax any physical tension that is being held in the body by softening the belly; relax the eyes and jaw and allow your shoulders to naturally fall away from the head.

After a short period of settling into present-time awareness, begin to reflect on your deepest desire for happiness and freedom from suffering. Allow your heart's sincere longing for truth and well-being to come into consciousness. With each breath, breathe into the heart's center the acknowledgment of your wish to be free from harm, safe, protected, and to experience love and kindness.

Slowly begin to offer yourself kind and friendly phrases with the intention to uncover the heart's sometimes-hidden loving and kind response. Your phrases can be as simple as the following:

"May I be happy."
"May I be at peace."
"May I be free from suffering."

If those phrases do not mean anything to you, create your own words to meditate on. Find a few simple phrases that have a loving and kind intention, and slowly begin to offer these well wishes to yourself.

As you sit in meditation repeating these phrases in your mind, the attention will be drawn back, as in mindfulness meditation, into thinking about other things or resisting and judging the practice or your capacity for love. It takes a gentle and persistent effort to return to the next phrase each time the attention wanders:

> "May I be happy." Feel the breath and the body's response to each phrase.
> "May I be at peace." Notice where the mind goes with each phrase.
> "May I be free from suffering." Allow the mind and body to relax into the reverberations of each phrase.

Simply repeat these phrases over and over to yourself like a kind of mantra or statement of positive intention. But don't expect to instantly feel loving or kind as result of this practice. Sometimes all we see is our lack of kindness and the judging mind's resistance. Simply acknowledge what is happening and continue to repeat the phrases, being as friendly and merciful with yourself as possible in the process.

After a few minutes of sending these loving and kind phrases to yourself, bring attention back to your breath and body, again relaxing into the posture.

Then bring someone to mind who has been beneficial for you to know or know of, someone who has inspired you or shown you great kindness. Recognizing that just as you wish to be happy and at peace that benefactor too shares the universal desire for well-being and love, begin offering him or her the loving and kind phrases. Slowly repeat each phrase with that person in mind as the object of your well-wishing:

"Just as I wish to be happy, peaceful, and free, may you too
   be happy."
"May you be at peace."
"May you be free from suffering."

Continue offering these phrases from your heart to your
benefactor's, developing the feeling of kindness and response
of love to others. When the mind gets lost in a story, memory,
or fantasy, simply return to the practice. Begin again offering
loving-kindness to the benefactor.

After a few minutes of sending loving-kindness to the benefactor, let him or her go and return to your direct experience of
the breath and body. Pay extra attention to your heart or emotional experience.

Then bring to mind someone whom you do not know well,
someone who is neutral. Someone you neither love nor hate—
perhaps someone you don't know at all, a person you saw
during your day, walking down the street or in line at the
market. With the understanding that the desire for happiness
and love is universal, begin offering that neutral person your
loving-kindness phrases:

"May you be happy."
"May you be at peace."
"May you be free from suffering."

After a few minutes of sending loving-kindness to the neutral
person, bring attention back to your breath and body. Then
expand the practice to include family and friends toward whom
your feelings may be mixed, both loving and judgmental:

"May you be happy."
"May you be at peace."
"May you be free from suffering."

After a few minutes of sending loving-kindness to the mixed category, bring attention back to your breath and body. Then expand the practice to include the difficult people in your life and in the world. (By *difficult* I mean those whom you have put out of your heart, those toward whom you hold resentment.)

With even the most basic understanding of human nature, it will become clear that all beings wish to be met with love and kindness; all beings—even the annoying, unskillful, violent, confused, and unkind—wish to be happy. With this in mind and with the intention to free yourself from hatred, fear, and ill will, allow someone who is a source of difficulty in your mind or heart to be the object of your loving-kindness meditation.

Meeting that person with the same phrases, pay close attention to your heart-mind's response:

"May you be happy."
"May you be at peace."
"May you be free from suffering."

After a few minutes of practice in the direction of difficult people, begin to expand the field of loving-kindness to all those who are in your immediate vicinity. Start by sending phrases of loving-kindness to anyone in your home or building at the time of practice. Then gradually expand to those in your town or city, allowing your positive intention for meeting everyone with love and kindness to spread out in all directions.

Imagine covering the whole world with these positive thoughts. Send loving-kindness to the north and south, east and west. Radiate an open heart and fearless mind to all beings in existence—those above and below, the seen and the unseen, those being born and those who are dying. With a boundless and friendly intention, begin to repeat the phrases:

"May all beings be happy."
"May all beings be at peace."
"May all beings be free from suffering."

After a few minutes of sending loving-kindness to all beings everywhere, simply let go of the phrases and bring attention back to your breath and body, investigating the sensations and emotions that are present now. Then, whenever you are ready, allow your eyes to open and your attention to come back to your surroundings.

APPRECIATIVE JOY MEDITATION

Find a comfortable place to sit, and allow your attention to settle into the present-time experience of the body. Relax any physical tension that is being held in the body by softening the belly; relax the eyes and jaw and allow the shoulders to naturally fall away from the head.

After a short period of settling into present-time awareness, begin to reflect on your deepest desire for happiness or freedom from suffering. Allow your heart's truest longing for truth and well-being to come into consciousness. With each breath, breathe into the heart's center the acknowledgment and appreciation of the joy and happiness you have experienced in your life.

Slowly begin to offer yourself appreciative and encouraging phrases with the intention to uncover the heart's sometimes-hidden response of gratitude. Your phrases can be as simple as the following:

"May I learn to appreciate the happiness and joy I experience."
"May the joy I experience continue and grow."
"May I be filled with gratitude."

If those phrases do not mean anything to you, create your own words to meditate on. Find a few simple phrases that have an appreciative intention, and slowly begin to offer these well wishes to yourself.

As you sit in meditation repeating these phrases in your mind, the attention will be drawn, as with mindfulness meditation, back into thinking about other things or resisting and judging the practice or your own capacity for appreciation and gratitude. It takes a gentle and persistent effort to return to the next phrase each time the attention wanders:

> "May I learn to appreciate the happiness and joy I experience." Feel the breath and the body's response to each phrase.
> "May the joy I experience grow." Notice where the mind goes with each phrase.
> "May I be filled with gratitude." Allow the mind and body to relax into the reverberations of each phrase.

Simply repeat these phrases over and over to yourself like a kind of mantra or statement of positive intention. But don't expect to instantly feel grateful through this practice. Sometimes all we see is our lack of appreciation and the judging mind's resistance. Simply acknowledge what is happening and continue to repeat the phrases, being as friendly and merciful with yourself as possible in the process.

After a few minutes of sending these phrases of appreciation to yourself, bring the attention back to the breath and body, again relaxing into the posture.

Then bring someone to mind who has been beneficial for you to know or know of, who has inspired you or brought joy to your life. Recognizing that just as you wish to be happy and successful in life that benefactor too shares the universal desire to be met with encouragement, support, and appreciation, begin offering him or her the phrases. Slowly repeat each phrase with that person in mind as the object of your well-wishing:

"Just as I wish to learn to appreciate the happiness and joy
   in life, may you too experience joy, and may you be
   filled with appreciation for your happiness and success."
"May your happiness and joy increase."
"May you be successful and met with appreciation."

Continue offering these phrases from your heart to your
benefactor's, developing the feeling of appreciation in relationship to the joy and success of others. When the mind gets lost in
a story, memory, or fantasy, simply return to the practice. Begin
again offering appreciation and gratitude to the benefactor.

After a few minutes of sending appreciation to the benefactor, let him or her go and return to your direct experience of
the breath and body. Pay extra attention to your heart or emotional experience.

Then bring to mind someone that you do not know well,
someone who is neutral. Someone you neither love nor hate—
perhaps someone you don't know at all, a person you saw
during your day, walking down the street or in line at the
market. With the understanding that the desire for joy is universal, begin offering that person the appreciative phrases:

"May your happiness and joy increase."
"May the joy in your life continue and grow."
"May you be successful and met with appreciation."

After a few minutes of sending appreciation to the neutral
person, bring attention to your breath and body. Then expand
the practice to include family and friends toward whom your
feelings may be mixed, both loving and judgmental:

"May your happiness and joy increase."
"May the joy in your life continue and grow."
"May you be successful and met with appreciation."

After a few minutes of sending appreciation to the mixed category, bring attention back to your breath and body. Then expand the practice to include the difficult people in your life and in the world. (By *difficult* I mean those whom you have put out of your heart, those toward whom you hold resentment.)

With even the most basic understanding of human nature, it will become clear that all beings wish to be met with appreciation; all beings—even the annoying, unskillful, violent, confused, and unkind—wish to experience joy. With this in mind, and with the intention to free yourself from jealousy, fear, and ill will, allow someone who is a source of difficulty in your mind or heart to be the object of your appreciation meditation. Meet that person with the same phrases, paying close attention to your heart-mind's response:

"May your happiness and joy increase."
"May the joy in your life continue and grow."
"May you be successful and met with appreciation."

After a few minutes of practice in the direction of difficult people, begin to expand the field of appreciation to all those who are in your immediate vicinity. Start by sending phrases of appreciation to anyone in your home or building at the time of practice. Then gradually expand to those in your town or city, allowing your positive intention for meeting everyone with appreciation to spread out in all directions.

Imagine covering the whole world with these positive thoughts. Send appreciation to the north and south, east and west. Radiate gratitude and appreciation to all beings in existence—those above and below, the seen and the unseen, those being born and those who are dying. With a boundless and friendly intention, begin to repeat the phrases of appreciative joy:

"May your happiness and joy increase."
"May the joy in your life continue and grow."
"May you be successful and met with appreciation."

After a few minutes of sending appreciation to all beings everywhere, simply let go of the phrases and bring attention back to your breath and body, investigating the sensations and emotions that are present now. Then, whenever you are ready, allow your eyes to open and your attention to come back to your surroundings.

EQUANIMITY MEDITATION

Find a comfortable place to sit, and allow your attention to settle into the present-time experience of the body. Relax any physical tension that is being held in the body by softening the belly; relax the eyes and jaw and allow your shoulders to naturally fall away from the head.

After a short period of settling into present-time awareness, begin to reflect on your deepest desire for happiness and freedom from suffering for both yourself and others. Reflect on your desire to serve the needs of others and to be compassionately engaged in the world. Reflect on both the joy and the sorrow that exist in the world. Allow your heart's truest longing for truth and well-being to come into consciousness. With each breath, breathe into the heart's center the acknowledgment of the need to balance your pure intention of creating positive change with the reality of your inability to control others.

Begin repeating the following phrases:

"All beings are responsible for their own actions."
"Suffering or happiness is created through one's relationship to experience, not by experience itself."
"The freedom and happiness of others is dependent on their actions, not on my wishes for them."

Relax into the reverberations of this balance between harmonizing the heart's deepest desire to help others with the mind's wise response of acknowledging our limitations and powerlessness.

Continue to repeat these phrases for as long as feels appropriate. Perhaps ten to twenty minutes is a good amount of time to start with.

FORGIVENESS MEDITATION

For this formal forgiveness practice it may be good to create an altar. It could be just a corner of the room, for example, or a small table where you place some photographs or objects that remind you of your intention to forgive.

Find a comfortable place to sit. Relax into the sitting posture. Take a few moments to settle into the position by intentionally releasing any held tension in your face, neck, shoulders, chest, or abdomen.

Bring your attention to the present moment through the breath awareness practice.

After settling into the present-time experience of sitting with awareness of the breath, allow the breath to come and go from your heart's center. Imagine breathing directly in and out of your heart. Feel what is present in your heart-mind and begin to set your intention to let go of the past through letting go of resentments. Say the word *forgiveness* in your mind and acknowledge how it feels to consider letting go.

When you are ready, bring to mind some of the ways that you have harmed others, have betrayed or abandoned them. Include both the intentional and unintentional acts of harm you have participated in. Acknowledge and feel the anger, pain, fear, or confusion that motivated your actions.

Begin to ask for forgiveness from those you have harmed:

"I ask for your forgiveness."

"Please forgive me for having caused you harm."

"I now understand that I was unskillful and that my actions hurt you, and I ask for your forgiveness."

Pause between each phrase, bringing attention to your heart/ mind/body's reactions to these practices. Feel the feelings that arise, or the lack of feeling. Acknowledge the desire to be forgiven. If the mind gets too lost in the story and begins rationalizing and blaming, simply bring your attention back to the breath and body in the present moment, then begin repeating the phrases:

"I ask for your forgiveness"
"Please forgive me for having caused you harm."
"I now understand that I was unskillful and that my actions
    hurt you, and I ask for your forgiveness"

Spend some time repeating these phrases and reflecting on your past unskillfulness, remembering to soften your belly when it gets tight with judgment or fear.

When you are ready, let go of the reflection on those you have harmed and bring your awareness back to yourself.

Relax back into breathing in and out of your heart's center. Take a few moments to let go of the last aspect of the exercise.

When you are ready, begin to reflect on yourself. Acknowledge all of the ways that you have harmed yourself. Contemplate your life and your thoughts, feelings, and actions toward yourself. Allow a heartfelt experience of the judgmental and critical feelings you carry toward yourself.

Just as we have harmed others, there are so many way that we have hurt ourselves. We have betrayed and abandoned ourselves many times, through our thoughts, words, and deeds—sometimes intentionally, often unintentionally.

Begin to feel the physical and mental experience of sorrow and grief for yourself and the confusion in your life. Breathing into each moment, with each feeling that arises, soften and begin to invite yourself back into your heart. Allow forgiveness to arise.

Picture yourself now, or at any time in your life, and reflect on all of the ways in which you have judged, criticized, and caused emotional or physical harm to yourself. With as much mercy and compassion as possible, begin to offer yourself forgiveness, perhaps picturing yourself as a child and inviting the disowned aspects of yourself back into your heart:

"I forgive you."
"I forgive you for all of the ways that you have caused me harm."
"I now offer you forgiveness, whether the hurt came through my actions, thoughts, or words."
"I know I am responsible for my actions, and I offer myself forgiveness."

Pause between each phrase, bringing attention to your heart/mind/body's reactions to these practices. Feel the feelings that arise, or the lack of feeling. Acknowledge the desire to be forgiven. If the mind gets too lost in the story and begins rationalizing and blaming, simply bring the attention back to the breath and body in the present moment, then begin repeating the phrases:

"I forgive you."

"I forgive you for all of the ways that you have caused me
    harm."
"I now offer you forgiveness, whether the hurt came
    through my actions, thoughts, or words."
"I know I am responsible for my actions, and I offer myself
    forgiveness."

Relax back into breathing in and out of your heart's center.
Take a few moments to let go of the last aspect of the exercise.

Then begin to reflect on all of the ways in which you have
been harmed in this lifetime. Remember that you are attempting to forgive the actors, not the actions, and that just as you
have been confused and unskillful at times, those who have
hurt you were also suffering or confused.

Bring to mind and invite back into your heart those who
have caused you harm. With as much mercy and compassion
as possible, begin offering forgiveness to those who have
harmed you, those whom you have been holding resentment
toward, with these same phrases:

"I forgive you."
"I forgive you for all of the ways that you have caused me
    harm."
"I now offer you forgiveness, whether the hurt came
    through your actions, thoughts, or words."
"I know you are responsible for your actions, and I offer
    you forgiveness."

Pause between each phrase, bringing attention to your heart/
mind/body's reactions to these practices. Feel the feelings that

arise, or the lack of feeling. Acknowledge the desire to forgive. If the mind gets too lost in the story and begins rationalizing and blaming, simply bring the attention back to the
breath and body in the present moment, then begin repeating
the phrases:

"I forgive you."
"I forgive you for all of the ways that you have caused me
   harm."
"I now offer you forgiveness, whether the hurt came
   through your actions, thoughts, or words."
"I know you are responsible for your actions, and I offer
   you forgiveness."

After some time of asking for forgiveness, let go of the
phrases and bring attention back to your direct experience of
the present moment, feeling the breath as it comes and goes,
softening the belly, and relaxing into the present.

Attempt to let go of all levels of this exercise, relaxing back
into the experience of your breath at the heart's center.

Send yourself a moment of gratitude for trying to free yourself from the long-held resentments that make life more difficult than it needs to be.

When you are ready, allow your eyes to open and attention
to come back into the room or space you are in.

REFLECTION ON DEATH MEDITATION

Sitting or lying down in a comfortable place, allow your eyes to close, and relax into the present-time experience. Feel your breath as it comes and goes. Notice the heaviness of the physical body, the pressure against the cushion or floor. Feel the effects of gravity on your body.

Begin to imagine or visualize your body as a corpse. See your body as motionless and inanimate. Acknowledge that this is the inevitable destiny of the body, and breathe in and out of the place of acceptance of death.

Now begin to see your body as dead for several days, bloated and beginning to rot. Imagine your body as lifeless and in an advanced stage of decomposition. Allow your imagination to be as graphic as you'd like—worms eating your flesh, maggots, etc.

Then move on to seeing your body as a skeleton, all of the flesh and blood gone, bones and ligaments alone remaining. Even the bones are beginning to crumble, eventually falling apart and scattering until finally only dust remains.

After some time, allow the reflection to end and return to mindfulness of your breath and body in the present moment.

ADVANCING ON
THE PATH TO FREEDOM

As you progress on the path to spiritual freedom, you will gain mastery of the practices outlined in this appendix. You will find yourself moving from rebel, to revolutionary, to radical as more and more you practice the Buddha's teachings.

THE REBEL'S PATH

The spiritual rebel does all of the following:

Meditates at least thirty minutes daily (including both wisdom and compassion practices)

Attends one residential meditation retreat a year

Follows the five precepts (don't kill, don't steal, don't use drugs, don't lie, and refrain from sexual misconduct)

Participates in a weekly meditation group

THE REVOLUTIONARY'S PATH

The spiritual revolutionary does all of the following:

Meditates at least one hour daily (focusing deeply on forgiveness and compassion practices for a period of five years)

Attends more than one retreat a year

Follows the five precepts

Commits life's-energy to a service-oriented profession

Participates in a weekly meditation group

THE RADICAL'S PATH

The spiritual radical does all of the following:

Meditates more than one hour daily (systematically train-ing in the wisdom and compassion practices)

Follows the five precepts

Commits life's-energy to a service-oriented profession

Participates in a weekly meditation group

Takes vows of celibacy for long periods of time

Attends longer silent retreats yearly (committing to one- to three-month intensive practice periods)

Begins, after ten years of deep practice, to share the dharma with others

RESOURCES

Suggested Reading in Nonfiction and Fiction, Web Resources, and Meditation Centers

SUGGESTED READING

Smith, Huston, and Philip Novak. *Buddhism: A Concise Introduction* (read this book first to get an honest overview of Buddhism).

Levine, Stephen. *Gradual Awakening.*

———. *A Year to Live.*

Levine, Stephen, and Ondrea Levine. *Who Dies?*

———. *Embracing the Beloved.*

Kornfield, Jack. *A Path with Heart.*

———. *After the Ecstasy the Laundry.*

———. *Teachings of the Buddha.*

Nanamoli, Bhikkhu. *The Life of the Buddha.*

Thera, Nyanaponika. *The Heart of Buddhist Meditation.*

Cha, Ajahn. *Food for the Heart.*

Salzberg, Sharon. *Loving-kindness.*

———. *A Heart as Wide as the World.*

———. *Faith.*

Goldstein, Joseph. *Insight Meditation.*

———. *One Dharma.*

Epstein, Mark. *Going to Pieces without Falling Apart.*

———. *Thoughts without a Thinker.*

Griffin, Kevin. *One Breath at a Time* (on Buddhism and the twelve steps).

Winston, Diana. *Wide Awake* (for teenagers).

Mahayana Perspective

Thurman, Robert. *Inner Revolution.*
Hahn, Thich Nhat. *The Miracle of Mindfulness.*
Roshi, Suzuki. *Zen Mind, Beginner's Mind.*

Novels

Hesse, Hermann. *Siddhartha.*
Crane, George. *Bones of the Master.*
Kerouac, Jack. *Dharma Bums.*

WEB RESOURCES

www.dharmapunx.com
www.againstthestream.com
www.accesstoinsight.org

MEDITATION CENTERS

WEST COAST

California

Spirit Rock Meditation Center
www.spiritrock.org
(415) 488-0164

Abhayagiri Buddhist Monastery
www.abhayagiri.org
(707) 485-1630

Oregon

Breitenbush Hot Springs Retreat Center
www.breitenbush.com
(503) 854-3320

Washington

Cloud Mountain Retreat Center
www.cloudmountain.org
(360) 274-4859

SOUTHWEST

New Mexico

Upaya Zen Center
www.upaya.org
(505) 986-8518

EAST COAST

Massachusetts

Insight Meditation Society and
Barre Center for Buddhist Studies
www.dharma.org
(978) 355-4378

Kripalu Yoga Retreat Center
www.kripalu.org
(866) 200-5203

New York

Menla Mountain Retreat Center
www.tibethouse.org
(212) 807-0563

Omega Institute
www.eomega.org
(845) 266-4444

To find local meditation groups, do a Web search in your area, using key words such as *insight meditation, Vipassana,* and *Theravadan.* I recommend teachers that are affiliated with the Spirit Rock Meditation Center or the Insight Meditation Society. Please be wise and careful in choosing which group(s) to join.

THANX!

Thanx to all my teachers. Especially Stephen and Ondrea Levine, Jack Kornfield, and Ajahn Amaro. And I offer deep gratitude to all my teachers' teachers, especially Ajahn Cha. Without the lineage of Buddhist practitioners that leads all the way back to Sid, I would have drowned long ago in the sea of samsara. Thanx for throwing me this raft.

Up the Punx! The roots of my spiritual rebellion began with the revolutionary punk rock movement. Respect to all the punx: those living and dead, those who are waking up, and those who are still napping.

Thanx to my editor, Eric Brandt, at HarperSanFrancisco. Your guidance was incredibly helpful.

Thanx to my literary agent, Loretta Barrett. May our association continue for years to come.

Thanx to the World Wide Dharma Punx Crew, especially the NYC, SF, and LA chapters. I deeply appreciate all of your support over the years. Keep the Faith. Destroy all Delusions.